FRIGATE BIRDS

Forty Years With the Solomons

Margaret Atkin

Published in Australia by Sid Harta Books & Print Pty Ltd,
ABN: 34632585293
23 Stirling Crescent, Glen Waverley, Victoria 3150 Australia
Telephone: +61 3 9560 9920, Facsimile: +61 3 9545 1742
E-mail: author@sidharta.com.au

First published in Australia 2023
Copyright © Margaret Atkin 2023
Cover design, typesetting: WorkingType (www.workingtype.com.au)

The right of Margaret Atkin to be identified as the Author of the Work
has been asserted in accordance with the Copyright, Designs and Patents Act 1988.

All rights reserved. No part of this publication may be reproduced,
stored in a retrieval system, or transmitted, in any form or by any means without the prior
written permission of the publisher, nor be otherwise circulated in any form of binding or cover
other than that in which it is published and without a similar condition being imposed on the
subsequent purchaser.

Margaret Atkin
Frigate Birds:
ISBN: 978-0-6484916-3-7
pp338

*To my father Ray Lycette for keeping my letters,
and to the women and girls of the Solomon Islands*

margaretatkin.com

Preface

Frigate birds live on rocky islands and emerge during high winds and storms to ride the currents. Carved on the prows of canoes, they watch out for enemies and spirits and provide inspiration for Solomon Islanders. In this deeply Christian country, they are found in many churches. Like them, much of my family's experience in the Solomons has been stormy; but, like them, we have learnt to ride the currents.

George Atkin and I were married in 1976 in Tawatana, Makira, after meeting at Wellington Polytechnic. He was studying journalism, while I was a nursing student. It was a profound shock to arrive in the village by canoe to be greeted by naked children and bare-breasted women. We washed in the stream, fetched water from the river and toileted in the sea. I was the only European at our wedding and our only present was a shell.

Quite rightly the Solomon Islands Nursing Registration Board decreed I was too inexperienced to register so I returned to NZ to obtain more experience and a midwifery diploma. George subsequently joined me.

We returned in 1977, a year before independence. George established the *Solomons Toktok*, the first independent weekly paper, while I worked as a nurse and nurse educator. George said in his independence issue that the Solomons wasn't ready for independence, and he was right.[1]

Because of the paper and George's connection with his cousin, Solomon Mamaloni, three times prime minister, we were always in the thick of politics.

In 1982, despite our financial insecurity, I joined George on the newspaper. I was rewarded with an extraordinary view of a society on the edge of change. Choices were still available, one of the most critical being effective family planning.

The Duke of Edinburgh commented on this during his visit with the Queen in 1983 declaring that with a birth rate of 3.4 per cent - one of the highest in the world - the people must be mad.[2]

The politicians were not concerned, apart from Sir Peter Kenliorea,[3] while the Solomon Islands Broadcasting Corporation broadcast a bulletin proclaiming an injectable contraceptive, Depo-provera, caused cancer.[4] Family planning was not widely adopted and the Solomons now has a population pyramid, with seven out of ten people under the age of thirty. This has strained the infrastructure and health and education sectors, while youth unemployment exceeds thirty-five per cent.[5]

Under Mamaloni, prime minister between 1981 and 1984, log exports quadrupled.[6]

Again, there was a choice. Following a field visit in 1976,

consultants from the United Nations Food and Agriculture Organisation recommended that a Solomon Islands Forestry Commission be set up.[7] As an intermediary, a commission could ensure companies had security while landowners got a fair deal.

This advice was ignored and under new legislation drafted in 1982, landowners set up their own logging companies. When there was a land dispute, the timber company had no security. This favoured logging companies and exploitation. They landed equipment from their barges, and if there was a major land dispute, pulled out. Fiji followed a different path, setting up the Fiji Pine Commission in 1976. This established a sustainable and profitable logging industry.[8]

While I was in NZ in mid-1983 on a three-month journalism scholarship, the marriage began to break down. I fled from the Solomons in early 1984 with our two children, Brian and John, then aged four and two. After a brief stay in Hong Kong with my parents, we resettled in Wellington where I worked as a journalist.

I have spent some of the happiest days of my life in the Solomons and have lifelong friendships.

My first trip alone back to Tawatana in early 1978 was an extraordinary experience. I was accepted and appreciated in a way I never had been before. In the Solomons, in 1983, I reviewed a book called *Mi Mere* in pidgin, meaning I am woman.[9] Reading this review forty years later my empathy and love for these women is evident.

It was this passion that drove me back to the Solomons in December 1998 to investigate the cervical cancer situation, which along with breast cancer is a major cause of death in Solomon Islands women. I did this for a master's thesis. George's eldest sister, Pepertua, died of it in 1997. It seemed unjust that I, who had the same early cellular abnormality, could access treatment and live, while she couldn't. There was little that could be done then. This changed when Gardasil, or HPV vaccine, became available in Australia in 2006.

A visiting Solomon Islands pathologist, Dr Roger Maraka, and I met Joe Tooma, the CEO of the Australian Cervical Cancer Foundation (ACCF) in March 2009. Joe was supportive and the ACCF put a proposal to the Solomon Islands Government that ACCF support the country prepare an application to GAVI (Global Vaccine Alliance Initiative) for a pilot cervical cancer vaccine project. This was accepted and in June 2013, Joe, I and my son Brian, who was then an IT manager, flew to the Solomons.

ACCF recruited a local nurse as the program supervisor and I became coordinator. We worked together with many Solomon Islands stakeholders, international organisations and an overseas consultant, Dr Scott La Montagne.

The application was accepted by GAVI in 2014, the pilot was successful and the Gardasil vaccine was introduced into the Solomons' national vaccine schedule in 2019.

In 2015, Family Planning Australia was invited by the Solomon Islands government to introduce a pilot cervical visual inspection screening and treatment program around Honiara and in Isabel province. This too was successful and has now been rolled out nationally.

While I was there in 2015, I noticed how difficult it was to eat well in Honiara. Fruit and vegetables were very expensive and it was harder to get fresh fish. The Chinese restaurants and shops had squeezed out the local competition with cheap, highly processed packaged food and now there is a diabetics diabetes epidemic. In 2021, the Solomons Islands had the sixth highest rate of diabetes in the world with twenty per cent of the population affected. Tahiti is the highest in the world at twenty-five per cent. Diabetes in Australia is around six to seven per cent.[10]

During his visit for the pilot vaccine launch in 2015, Brian was asked by his cousin Ronnie to help create a business for the family. He created Makira Gold, a social business and cacao export company. Solomon Islands cacao farmers, using the latest drying and transport techniques, export hyphenated top-class beans to artisan chocolate makers in Australia and Europe. While our generation attempted to establish a successful business for years without success, the next generation has finally succeeded.

After continuing as a print and radio journalist, George went on to work as a media or press secretary for successive prime ministers. Much has been written about the Solomon Islands by outsiders, but there are few books by Solomon Islanders. I hope George's memoir will be one of the next.

CONTENTS

Preface		iii
Chapter 1	Meeting and marriage in Tawatana	1
Chapter 2	Student apprentice nurse, tawatana and independence	15
Chapter 3	Mum's visit, sedition, cyclones and pregnancy	35
Chapter 4	Brian's birth, school of nursing	53
Chapter 5	Pregnancy, John's birth and leaving nursing	69
Chapter 6	Journalism cadet	83
Chapter 7	NZ training, return to Solomons and flight	115
Chapter 8	Back to the Solomons with the children	145
Chapter 9	Cervical cancer – a pilot study	181
Chapter 10	The 'Tension' and Brian and Meredith's wedding	195
Chapter 11	Chinatown burns and logging in Tawatana	215

Chapter 12	The walk up the Makira Coast and HIV education	229
Chapter 13	Introduction of cervical cancer vaccine and Isabel	247
Chapter 14	Honiara preparation, vaccine launch, screening and treatment	265
Chapter 15	Makira Gold – from cacao farmers to artisan chocolate makers	273
Chapter 16	Catching up	285
Afterword		307
Bibliography		313
End Notes		319

Chapter 1

MEETING AND MARRIAGE IN TAWATANA

When a Black man with a halo of corkscrew curls sat uninvited at our table at the Wellington Polytechnic cafe, I didn't know my life was about to change. While we shivered in our jackets and jerseys in the winter of 1975, he wore a tee shirt. He put down his tray, loaded with roast chicken and chips, and as we demurely munched our sandwiches introduced himself.

This was George Atkin, a Solomon Islands radio journalist, his English surname self-chosen in honour of Joseph Atkin. Joseph was an English missionary martyred alongside Bishop Patteson in 1871 in Santa Cruz. It was a revenge killing following the previous kidnapping of five islanders by blackbirders. George told us his middle name was 'One', the Arosi word for sand beach where his mother had given birth to him. She had been caught short during her four-hour walk to the clinic.

George looked like the way out of the middle-class New Zealand life I found so boring. My family was worried, not because he was a Melanesian, but because he was George, with a history of womanising and drinking. Undeterred, I pushed ahead, buying a cream ankle-length dress from Vinnies and a pair of white sandals. We bought two rings and booked for the Solomons.

In December 1975, we circled down through the clouds to the green hills and leaf huts surrounding Honiara. The heat and humidity immediately hit me as we left the plane and walked across the tarmac to the shed. This was no tourist destination. The other passengers were Solomon Islanders and a few returning residents, Europeans and Chinese. The airline clerk looked at me curiously and while George kept greeting people, I felt uneasy. We were picked up by a European, George's boss.

The sea and sky were grey, and I peered into cavernous shed-like shops, while at their roadside stalls Solomon Islanders sold green coconuts and bananas. The road was potholed, most of the cars were belching fumes and the taxis looked particularly dilapidated. Tall, spindly coconut trees riddled with bullet holes, hedged the sea.

The next shock was George's house. It was tiny, a fibreboard house on stilts in a sea of mud in a muddy road among others like it. There were three small bare rooms, a toilet and a shower where I did our washing in a bucket.

The next day I accompanied George to his interview with the chief minister, his cousin Solomon Mamaloni, the pre-independence equivalent of prime minister. He was a short man, bright and wily, his mouth stained red with betel nut, regarded with suspicion by some expatriate bureaucrats.

My father and I had met Mamaloni earlier that year in New Zealand, accompanied by a European dad regarded as unsavoury. It was this association, and a deal to have commemorative coins struck without government approval, which forced Mamaloni's resignation the following year. Mamaloni told George he would be sent to the West, a beautiful part of the Solomons with reefs and atolls.[11]

The following day we flew in a small plane to Makira, George's home island, where we planned to spend Christmas with his family. Kirakira, the provincial capital, was pretty, with its immaculate grass park and huge rainforest trees. The hospital, church, government offices and shops all bordered the park. The rivers were high and we had to wait a couple of days for them to drop.

When they did it was almost Christmas, so instead of walking for three days we got a lift in a large Bedford truck, accompanied by a grader. Inland, the country was hilly and covered with dense rainforest, with small villages scattered along the coast.

People lived in leaf huts alongside coconut plantations. The largest river was just before Macedonia, Mamaloni's village, and the grader spent half an hour levelling the riverbed before the Bedford breasted through. In Macedonia, they volunteered to take us the rest of the way by canoe, and on 24 December we were dropped at Tawatana.

Even now, I remember that landing. It was dusk and

the villagers were lined up along the beach, while the bush-covered hills loomed behind them. The women were bare-breasted and tattooed, and the children naked with skinny legs and big bellies. We caught a wave, and in the shallows they were upon us, lifting the bags out, helping me over the side and hauling the canoe up the shingle beach. There was the flicker of a few kerosene lamps. Up at the family hut on the plateau, I refused to be separated from George.

On Christmas Day, we feasted on pigs and taro pudding, which I found indigestible.

I wrote to my parents that George's parents, Basil Bunaone and Rebi, were aristocratic looking but didn't speak English and I felt lost. However, I did enjoy the large cool wooden huts on stilts with leaf roofs and bamboo floors and slept on a thin foam mattress I had bought in Kirakira. The food was challenging, with George finding the sweet potato and bush cabbage in coconut milk breakfast and dinner as monotonous as I did. George said I liked fruit, so that afternoon ten pineapples, numerous rock melons, ten pawpaws, sugar cane and ripe bananas were left on the verandah.

George's sister, Pepertua, had a boy of seven, Don, with a big belly and skinny legs. He was one of the children Rebi cared for. George wanted to take him to the clinic, four hours' walk away, but I thought there was little point as his intellectual and physical disability appeared permanent.[12]

Chapter 1 Meeting and marriage in Tawatana

✼

Sometimes we went picnicking with Rebi and took our place at the end of the line behind Don and the other small children. She was tall and slender, with a swaying gait and her pipe, made from an umbrella handle, clenched between her red stained teeth. She was always bare breasted with a skirt of indeterminate colour after years of being washed in muddy river water.

In her string bag she carried betelnut, a lime container, leaf and a stock of dried tobacco leaves. She also carried a machete and a coconut shell with a glowing ember. From this she lit fires and her pipe.

We took the steep track which dropped from the plateau through jagged coral reefs to the path beside the sea. There were caves, and people kept pigs down under the coconuts, building pens with coral.

Rebi picked up her bamboo and we followed the track to the river mouth and the small black sandy bay, Haurahu. Up this river, there were banana plantations and a spring.

On the rock platform on the other side of the river mouth was a blowhole with low cliffs behind it. Here they hunted coconut crabs at night. Around the corner, Rebi had planted pawpaws and pineapples. While she went fishing, either off the rocks or at the edge of the reef, the children played. Sometimes they cut themselves balsawood surfboards and rode the waves, while we hunted for hermit crabs to restock Rebi's bait.

When we were thirsty, a small boy hopped up a coconut tree with a machete. When we were hungry, we looked for sprouted coconuts and smashed them open, scooping out the yellow spongy sweet ball. George lit a fire and heated round river rocks in preparation for the fish.

In my diary, I wrote I was as useless as the smallest child. I was unable to handle a machete, climb a coconut tree, or carry a bucket of water on my head.

When the children laughed at me, George told me Rebi reprimanded them, saying I came from a different world. It was a world Rebi didn't know as she had never left Makira. I was told that when she went to Kirakira and saw her reflection in a glass window, she was terrified.

We ate in the late afternoon when it was cooler and there were fewer flies. Happy and full, we walked home and, as the sun set quickly, we carried bush torches, bundles of dry fronds to light our way.

The most difficult task was going down to the beach in the early morning to the women's toilet. I had to climb down the coral path to the sea, walk along to the women's area and squat behind a low log in the surf. In the early days, I misjudged the waves and got thoroughly soaked. Privacy was impossible as people were on the beach at first light.

One evening, I ate coconut crab and got diarrhoea. That night I had to pick my way down the steep sharp coral track to the sea. I decided whenever I returned, I would try to bring my own toilet.

Bathing was also challenging. I crept down to the stream

at night. This ran through the middle of the village and was downstream from the men's pool. I waded into the cool water and furtively scrubbed my private parts hoping no one was looking from the nearby open windows.

Another memory was the woman who giggled. This was Rosina, who had brain damage after she was hit on the head by her husband. She could no longer look after herself, let alone her two children. Her family cared for her children while she was fed by the village. A couple of years later, she disappeared.[13]

On New Year's Day, we began our four-day walk to Kirakira. George had to get to Honiara to cover a Legislative Assembly meeting.

We walked three hours to the village where George's Seventh Day Adventist relatives lived. Their feast of chicken and fish was much more to my taste than pork. Afterwards we kept walking along the beaches and through coconut plantations and villages, the dense rainforest always alongside us. There were quick, heavy downpours, with thunder and lightning and every night we reached a relative's hut.

One river was very high so we made a raft to float our packs and bags across. I hung on to onto it but midway lost my grip and was carried downstream. On the bank, George clutched a branch with one hand and with the other grabbed me as I floated past. The river mouths are known for crocodiles, the one creature that scares Solomon Islanders.

When we reached Kirakira it was strange to have

electricity again, although the diesel generator shut down at ten. The next day George left on the plane while I waited for a ship. I stayed in the rest house and was chaperoned by Evalyn, one of the older daughters of the Anglican priest and his wife.[14]

In Evalyn, aged 18, I had found my first Solomon Islands friend. I was always welcome at their house and if I didn't turn up they would come and fetch me. Evalyn and I talked for hours, went on picnics, went swimming, and I read books from the rest house. I read a lesson in church and watched mass being prepared for two prisoners.

I joked with a government official who spent a night telling me very funny stories and was invited by the senior European nurse to dinner where we dined on pork chops. People brought me bananas and I was invited to other houses for supper. I was very happy. I wrote that George and I had decided to return to Tawatana and get married on 23 January [(ibid)].

I caught a small boat on Friday with many other passengers. Because George's cousin knew the crew, I was given the only passenger cabin with four bunks. I was grateful as it was rough, even with seasick pills. They brought me food at lunchtime and lemon drink. The only thing I regretted was the ship's toilet wasn't working.

We stayed on an island overnight. Together with a

woman who had two children, I was housed at the priest's house. At noon, the boat picked us up again and we sailed for Honiara. We didn't arrive until 4 am. I was advised to lie down with the rest of the women, while the men sat up. The sea was very rough. One girl was seasick, but she stopped after I gave her two lots of seasick pills.

It was extraordinary to see the care of the crewman delegated to look after her. He emptied the bucket of salt water she threw up into. He held her hair back, so she didn't vomit into it and gave her sips of water. Again, fifteen hours without a lavatory. I was offered pudding but eventually chose to eat pineapple, bully beef and biscuits with some Tikopians. I wrote to my parents:

> One must endure things that would seem harder in NZ, but it's easier here because of the community spirit.
>
> Passing these fully bush covered islands, I find myself missing New Zealand, its paddocks and its space. Here, people are living with and in their environment while it still feels very foreign to me.[15]

Back in Honiara on 12 January I found the town unsettled. After the announcement of independence in July 1978, on 2 January the only union in the Solomons had gone on strike for better wages. Marchers smashed shop windows, threatened police, threw bottles into buses and ripped up food gardens. They said this was in response to the police who used tear gas.[16]

Mamaloni was touchy, not only about the union, but about the media. There was no independent radio or newspaper in the Solomons and news was provided by the Government Information Service. Initially, three expatriate journalists supported the journalists in the radio station and government newspaper, but two expatriates were dismissed. It was difficult for the one who remained to support the journalists and yet placate the chief minister.

I wrote that George was upset.

> He is reporting on the Legislative Assembly, which is the equivalent of our Parliament. After the sittings end in the afternoon, he goes back to the office and prepares his report. This must be approved and frequently changes are requested. George said that the officials didn't dare behave like this when the two expatriate journalists were there.
>
> Now, the local journalists feel unprotected. After a week he 'broke out' and organised a meeting with the other journalists. He thinks if he can get another job he will. Then he will rejoin the Solomon Islands Broadcasting Corporation (SIBC) when it is independent. This is part of the National Development Plan.[17]

We went back to the village to get married. I felt isolated and lonely. The women were afraid to speak with me as the men jeered at their attempts to speak English. I sulked, and read, wandered along the beach, and swam, one day in a storm with a high sea. I was being pulled out by the current when George's cousin scrambled around the rocky point and pulled me in.

A more pleasant memory was a walk with George's ten-year-old nephew. He pointed out things and while I said the English word, he would give the Arosi.

I wrote these down and attempted to continue my education with George. When he laughed at my pronunciation, I threw the notebook away.

We finally got married on 1 Feb 1976 at seven in the morning.

I was up before dawn and went to the beach to go to the toilet, trying to elude the endless stream of people. When I got to the church, it was packed, with crowds outside trying to peer in. They parted and I walked down the aisle alone and sat next to George in the front pew. Because I was not confirmed, I received a blessing like the children and two chiefs alongside me. We said our vows and went out the back to sign the book. George and I then stood outside and shook hands with many, many people. One man gave me a shell, remarking he knew it was the European custom to give presents.

We climbed the path to the plateau, near the school, for the feast. Everyone attending dropped a stone into a bucket and six hundred were counted. Numerous men climbed a rickety platform and gave speeches in Arosi. I was not asked to speak and couldn't have because it was against custom for a woman to be physically higher than a man.

I learnt later most of the speakers were sorry none of my family were present. At the feast, we ate thirteen pigs and taro pudding, both highly indigestible, and then watched men play soccer.

After taking a canoe to Kirakira and flying back to Honiara, I found a telegram from my parents. They advised me not to get married. I told them it was too late and described the wedding.[18]

The final letter to my parents was undated and described a local picnic:

> We hired two taxis and with four neighbours drove to a nearby river. Picnics were very busy affairs.
>
> First, Albert dashed off and erected a bush shelter while George and I gathered river stones that would not explode and made a fire.
>
> We put the chicken on the hot stones, added more stones on top, and covered them with banana leaves weighed down by sticks.
>
> The food was delicious. We also went swimming, my freestyle was admired, and we watched Albert diving and surfacing with a fish in his hands.[19]

That picnic haunted me when I had to return to chilly New Zealand. This was to gain more nursing experience and complete a midwifery diploma so I could register as a nurse in the Solomons. I also missed George, who had flown to Gizo to work with the Solomon Islands Broadcasting Corporation.

I got a job in a paediatric surgical ward at Wellington Hospital but after six months decided to move to New Plymouth. This was close to the family farm in Tikorangi, run by my maternal uncle, Bob, and his wife Sue. I worked in a medical ward and lived in the nurses' quarters. When I heard some Solomon Islands postgraduate nursing students were living in the old quarters, I shifted there. Finally, I made friends, including Jane and Mackay. Jane was a New Zealand enrolled nurse while Mackay was a Solomon Islands nurse.

George returned to NZ in late 1976 and found work as a government clerk in Wellington and we had Christmas in Wellington with my parents who were back from Hong Kong. It was good to be reunited with them and my three younger siblings.

In January 1977, I began a six-month midwifery diploma at Wellington Hospital and in mid-1977 George and I returned to the Solomons, this time for good.

Chapter 2

STUDENT APPRENTICE NURSE, TAWATANA AND INDEPENDENCE

I began work as a nurse in the labour ward of the National Hospital shortly after we arrived in July 1977. It was more relaxed than NZ as most women gave birth to six or more children. After a push and a grunt, the baby was usually out.[20] In late July, we were saddened by a maternal death. A woman was admitted with placenta praevia, her placenta blocking her vagina. She went straight to theatre and began to bleed but they only had two units of blood to give her. She was sent to the ward and died later that night.

Early in January 1978, I was sent to the emergency department. From the first day I was aware of my responsibility. If the wrong person, especially a child, was sent home they could be dead the next day. My priority was communication, and I was grateful to be living with many relatives because my pidgin improved rapidly.

I learnt quickly how to examine children and identify chest and ear infections, dehydration, malaria, dengue and meningitis. If concerned, I would consult the doctor in the end room. I learnt to suture and cannulate.

I wondered about the blood prick for malaria. It was a needle embedded in a cork and suspended in a bottle of alcohol which was used for everyone. Malaria was common with people often coming in shivering and intensely cold but with very high fevers. This was a medical emergency, and they were given IV quinine and admitted. However, people presented with varying symptoms and we always checked for it.

In children, chest infections were common with many also presenting with diarrhoea because of the poor water quality. Many had scabies and hookworm was common in adults and children, sometimes causing severe anemia.

I saw babies with neonatal tetanus infected because their cord had been cut with a sliver of wood and their mothers were unvaccinated. Luckily, the skilled pediatrician saved the majority. Mum said dad saw one such a case in Whakatane. It was regarded as so unusual that the case study was published in the international medical journal, the *Lancet*.

Another case I remember was the boy who overdosed on Panadol after a relationship breakup. He waited a few days before he presented and died of liver failure.

In those days, there were few presentations of lifestyle diseases such as diabetes, heart disease and high blood pressure. It was unusual to see an overweight person and most people, even in Honiara, still had access to traditional food such as sweet potatoes, yams and bush cabbage. There was also more fish and cheap canned tuna. Family from villages on the home islands often sent food baskets to their relatives in Honiara. Many people also had gardens up in the hills, near the squatter settlements.

George began the *Solomons Toktok* in 1977 and in an article for Griffith University he said running a weekly independent newspaper was tough. Not only did he have to gather and write news, but find advertising, take photos and cover sports. He then laid the paper out before it was printed and, after printing, delivered it, kept the accounts and did the banking.

It was a struggle professionally, financially and personally. As a previous broadcast journalist George was unused to providing captions and headlines. Government officials and politicians, who had never dealt with independent journalists, found it confronting, and there was not enough revenue to cover expenses.[21]

During my first leave in February 1978 I returned to Tawatana by boat. It was rough and after hours of pitching up and down and vomiting I clambered over the boat's side into a dinghy and went ashore. It was raining. I was greeted with cries of 'commander Margaret', meaning well done in pidgin. They appreciated I had come alone.

Because my pidgin had improved, I could speak with

people including Rebi, who 'heard' pidgin but was too ashamed to speak it. I was led to a small hut, away from the others, which I shared with George's paternal grandmother, Kaha or May. She was a very old and almost blind from cataracts. The hut leaked.

The weather improved and I began to enjoy myself with fishing and swimming. I had toughened up and was coping better with the relentless diet of kumara in coconut milk, sleeping on a mat and using the beach as a toilet.

I also finally found a friend, Ester, who had only three children compared to most who had from six to ten. Ester's husband, George, was an older, tolerant man who accepted our friendship.

I was Ester's shadow, following her to her garden in the bush, down to the river and to the sea. I was a poor student, struggling to find the tubers which led to sweet potatoes. We carried them home on our heads and I had a child's basket. Ester not only carried a much larger basket, she also often had a load of firewood strapped to her back.

I loved our time in the garden with the wonderful view of the bay. One day Ester found some bees and smoked them out. I got quite drunk on the fermented sweetness of the wild honey. Under Ester's tuition I chewed betelnut with lime powder and leaf, finding it bitter but relaxing. We burnt yams and drank green coconuts while Ester told me stories.

I learnt about cranes, one of their totems, kakamoras, the playful and mischievous dwarves in the bush, and the great sickness in the old days. Returning along a coastal path on dusk, I remember her calling to the spirit of the water in Arosi, to introduce me. She became a lifelong friend.

Another great companion was Casper. Unlike most people he remained unmarried. If you asked him why, he'd say, 'I never met the right woman' or 'I couldn't bear to be scolded all day.' Unlike the other village men he didn't leave early in the morning to build bush gardens, go hunting or work on copra.

He was never found at the communal workdays at the school, the cemetery or the church. He would only turn up, and that was on the fringe, when the village council threatened to fine him. Instead, he would stay in the village with the elderly and small children and so we had time to talk. We would sit on the verandah of his two-storey house and he would tell me stories.

He was the only one in the village with a two-storey house. He had seen a picture in a magazine and decided to build it. The others laughed at him and said the top floor would fall down but Casper was determined.

When he had built the upper floor the whole village gathered. Casper climbed up the ladder, walked around and jumped up and down on it. It held and the crowd went away disappointed. Slowly, he finished the upper walls and put up the sago-palm roof. When a cyclone struck five years later, his house was one of the few along the beach which was not destroyed.

He told me stories about the old days, about how the white men in their big boats shelled the villages along the coast. He said they were angry because the locals had killed a white plantation owner. He had been known for his cruelty and had beaten some of his labourers to death. I learnt more about this episode from Father Abel later.

Casper showed me an iron cannon ball, about the size of a tennis ball. He also told me about the shark worship, which was confirmed by George who said his grandfather had been a shark caller.

He took me to see the catamaran he had been building for years to sail around the Solomons. It was never finished, and he never left the village. It was as well because Michael Scott, an English anthropologist who arrived in the village in the early nineties relied on him as one of his informants.

I went into the bush with an old bushman, John, and saw sites even villagers had not seen before, including a burial mound. This was in a valley where there had once been a large village. There were deliberate cuts on some of the stones and wild bananas, sago palms and coconuts on the hillsides. The whole village had died of dysentery.

I saw the giant river stones a giant is reputed to have carried to the top of a hill for his oven. Nearby was a grotto where he washed himself in a small rock pool fed by a spring. He had too many enemies to drink at the river.

The Solomon Islanders were very happy in the bush,

while I was awed by the huge trees, the gloom and lack of undergrowth. I was shown edible trees and other bush food such as wild taros, turmeric and bush cabbage. There were vines that could be cut for water and trees to build houses, roofs, and canoes. It was often muddy underfoot so I went barefoot on steep hills where the path usually went straight up.

I walked two hours to see the only business in the area, a small furniture making venture. The owner made $250 in the past year making tables and chairs and said he would make more making copra but enjoyed what he was doing.

Meanwhile, George's father Basil, one of the three village chiefs, told me about the land disputes and the block of land he wanted to buy up the coast. This was the plantation later bought by Barnabas, which is now worked by Henry and his family. It was being sold then by a Chinese for $12,000. His family bought it for a case of tobacco!

I wrote to my parents that some people made money from copra and then didn't know what to do with it.

One highlight I described was my delivery of a chief's wife. It was her fifth child and she didn't have time to walk three hours to the clinic:

> We boiled a razor blade and the birth was a simple one. All the women could deliver babies, but as a midwife I was used to controlling the baby's head and after delivery, wrapping and handing the baby to the mother to suckle. This encouraged bonding and contractions,

so the placenta usually came out. I earned the name of 'commander' again. [22]

They asked me to work at the new clinic they were building with their own money. They had stopped paying taxes. Their councillor also recently received funds from the South Pacific Foundation for a village canoe. I said I was tempted but didn't want to be separated from George.

One of the last things I did before I left was to hold a meeting for the women in the area.

> Fifty women came. I asked why the women's clubs in the area are breaking down. They told me there was a shortage of leaders and space to hold meetings and little support from Kirakira and Honiara. They are very interested in family planning. Currently, many have eight to ten children. This is tough in an environment with no running water, no electricity, little money and food gardens half an hour to an hour's walk away. They have to carry the baby everywhere.[23]

It was strange to be back in Honiara, the house a mess with invitations lying about. George was becoming popular.[24]

I spent two miserable weeks in Honiara at home. I missed the village and unwisely we used money my parents loaned us for a house to buy an unreliable car.

George said he needed it to cover the independence celebrations in July. I was relieved when I finally boarded the boat to Malaita to join thirdyear nursing students for rural nursing experience.

I was on the ship all night. When I arrived at five, I was whipped away by the senior nursing officer for my first bacon and egg breakfast and hot shower since arriving in the Solomons. She was pleasant, dedicated, and experienced.

At eleven, the jeep finally arrived. They had been waiting for a spare tyre. All the available spares had punctures. Unlike Makira, there are roads here, although rough ones, and cattle grazing alongside.

The driver tried to tell me about the villages as we passed through, but the jeep rattled so much I couldn't hear him. We finally arrived at the substation Malu'u, 82 km from Auki, and at the northern tip of the island. I was greeted by five nursing students, three women and two men, and found the house far more comfortable than ours in Honiara. However, the food was unimpressive; rice, hard biscuits and cheap fatty corned beef.[25]

It was the weekend, a pretty place near the sea, but I quickly realised the people were different from those in Makira. An old man presented me with a shell in a red sock. I thought he was giving it to me, but no, he was selling it. The students and nurses said the people were aloof and didn't trust outsiders. The nurses are responsible for the health of 15,000 to 25,000 people in their clinic areas.

The next letter was sent from Bita'ama, 20 km closer to Auki.

I wrote it from a sago-palm hut, said I had eaten breakfast and was about to visit a school. The handover which should have taken a week was given in three hours late at night:

> Each morning people pour into the small clinic with their headaches, sores, and chest infections, although the afternoons are quiet and there is little afterhours work. There are very few deliveries as the women commonly deliver in their villages. The clinic has run out of essentials including tetanus vaccine, and eusol used for dressing wounds.[26]

I wrote that the previous day I had carried out a survey in a small village of seventeen huts. They were made of sago-palm, on stilts but had no windows.

In an interview with the schoolteacher, I learnt about an illegitimate baby, and an epileptic boy who kept fitting and falling into fires until he was finally medicated.[27]

I wrote again from Fauabu Hospital, a rambling mission hospital built in 1929 for leprosy patients. I was lying on a quilt-covered bed in a curtained cubicle listening to the chugging of a generator outside which ran until 10 o'clock.

After twenty-five years the roofs were falling down and the concrete walls cracking. I arrived on Monday to be greeted by Helen Barrett, the senior nurse who had been there since 1968 and been joined by two other European nurses.

We had to push start their jeep and as we were rattling along the road we were stopped by a man who said his wife having trouble giving birth.

We raced up to his village and into a hut with a dirt floor. The baby was out but the placenta was still in.

While the sister went to the jeep to get the Syntometrine injection, the placenta fell out. We then took her to the hospital for repair of her perineal tear. The baby must have fallen out too.

On the way, we stopped for another person. A child had fallen into a fire and was badly burned with third degree burns over a fifth of his body. We took him to Auki Hospital. His parents had thrown sugar over his burn. When Helen asked why, she was told it was to stop it 'boiling up.'

By 10.30 we were back for the child health and antenatal clinic. There were some sick babies, but most were healthy. The nurses knew the families and their histories well and were doing excellent work with family planning.

I have great admiration for these nurses especially since I've learnt their salary is less than mine. They may not be here for much longer though, as it is getting harder for Europeans to obtain work permits, and soon the provincial government will take over the hospital.[28]

The country owes a lot to people like this, and they

have been very kind to me. I have been eating European food for the first time in nine months. I will send them something when I get back to Honiara.[29]

A day later I was in Auki staying in a comfortable house with the senior nursing officer, Ms McDermot. She was committed and respected by her Solomon Islands' colleagues. She said whatever fix she got into, someone helped. She described arriving unexpectedly in a village for the night. The people carried a bed into her hut, followed by a mattress.

> I spent one day in the emergency department working with a doctor who taught me how to palpate for enlarged livers and spleens (malaria), how to feel for kidneys and look through peoples' pupils into their blood vessels. While he examined one patient, I examined another and asked him when I was unsure. I am slowly gathering confidence with so many people teaching me and am happier.[30]

When I got back we bought a two-bedroomed house in Vura, near a school and a shop, and on a bus run. It would take three years to pay off.

I was settling down in the emergency department, too.

During one busy shift, I referred a woman with possible mouth cancer, and another woman with possible rheumatic fever and a third with a headache. She thought it was caused by her new hair dye. Her blood pressure was 220 over 110.

George and I began to argue about my desire to retain my New Zealand citizenship. It became clearer as independence approached that the Solomons was not going to permit dual citizenship.[31]

A fortnight later we had moved into our new house and I described the government's preparations for independence, two months away. They were painting the hospital and the labourers' huts visible from the road, but not the others.[32]

> Over the weekend, George and I interviewed a Chinese hermit. He had been living in a small hut for more than twenty years, since 1956, supported not by the Chinese but his Solomon Islands neighbours.
>
> When we went to see him we took him some batteries for his radio and some newspapers. George invited him over for Sunday and we went and picked him up in the car. We cooked food in a stone oven. He is nice, if a little odd.
>
> He has a disconcerting habit of asking quick questions and then answering them himself, questions like, how long do cats live? He is a mine of information as he's been learning from discarded newspapers for about twenty years.[33]

In early June, I met the Australian eye team.

One surgeon who had been coming for nine years said

apart from the reduced incidence of trachoma the standard hadn't improved.

> We nurses are supposed to be giving intraconjunctival injections of penicillin after trauma. A lot of eyes have been lost because they get infected.[34]

In mid-June, on my day off, I was helping an old man dig a road behind the house to get our car up.

> I get amazed looks as people drive past and see a European woman attacking the ground with a pick. I got involved because I felt sorry for the old man who is very thin and has a bad leg. He has made a good job of the vegetable garden on top of the bank and planted cabbages, shallots and tomatoes.[35]

Independence loomed and preparations were well under way:

> I have never seen the town looking so flashy. The grass verges have been cut, there are Solomon Islands flags strewn across the road and coloured lights everywhere. People are practising marching and public toilets being built.[36]

Finally on Saturday, the royal representatives arrived.

Although I had barely three hours' sleep after night duty, I drove George out to the airport to watch, with two thousand other people, the Duke and Duchess of Gloucester arrive. Many of the locals walked three to four miles to get there.

The duke and duchess walked down the red carpet, the duchess was given flowers and the duke inspected the guard. But more interesting were the press. They had been arriving for a couple of days, from Australia, NZ, Japan Fiji and PNG. It was fascinating to watch them darting up and taking pictures.

A local boy pestered George about being his photographer, so George thought he'd give him a chance. He looked very nervous as the overseas photographers got themselves set up as the plane was taxiing in and said he needed to go to the toilet. He missed the whole thing. We picked him up walking back alongside the road.

> George has been invited to a couple of press functions but not to any of the social functions. He is rather cross. Today at 4 pm, the Australian Film Unit is coming to shoot George and his staff at work. There are two organisations paying him $200 each for coverage and they seem happy so far.[37]

George believed the Solomons was not ready for independence and wrote that people didn't understand democracy. I remember struggling to describe it to Basil:

> I have two newspapers published that day, the government

paper the *News Drum* and the *Solomons Toktok*. The *News Drum* had articles from the Governor-General Baddeley Devesi, the Prime Minister Peter Kenilorea, and a feature written by Tony Hughes, an expatriate and senior bureaucrat titled 'Challenges for the new nation'. He noted the nation needed a steady flow of agricultural, mining, timber and fishing projects and these, particularly the last two, it certainly got.

The *Toktok*, titled the 'Birth of a nation' had an article titled 'Unity in the country?' in which George wrote of the lack of national identity, with most Solomon Islanders identifying with their tribe and their island. George wrote of issues raised by the MP John Talasasa who led the Western Breakaway Movement formed in 1977.

They were concerned about land ownership, as sixty to eighty per cent of land in the West was owned by foreign companies, the government or by Solomon Islanders from other provinces. The Western Breakaway Movement was also concerned its their timber profits were subsidising poorer provinces.[38]

George also wrote that East and West Guadalcanal were thinking of expelling internal migrants, particularly Malaitans. It was this ongoing conflict that led to the failed state in 2002 and the subsequent RAMSI intervention in 2003.

In another article titled 'Solomons thereafter' George pointed out that the largest group in the House were independents with no party affiliation. After eighty-five years of British rule development had been concentrated in the urban areas, while ninety per cent of the population lived in the rural areas and contributed almost a third of the national economy.[39]

The day after independence I was relieved it was over and I finally had a day off. George had been congratulated on his independence issue by many of the overseas press.

On the evening of the sixth, I went to the ceremony which consisted of the lowering of the British flag. Straining over the heads of ten thousand people, it was a difficult to see but I got a few glimpses of the parade, the marching girls and the bands. George was in the grandstand.

They had a fifteen-minute fireworks display which was very loud, very smoky and rained ashes on everyone. The children were terrified and George left early because he said it reminded him too much of World War II.

> Yesterday was independence and I was working hard. There was a staff shortage but not a shortage of patients, some acute. We had one man with a perforated gastric ulcer, his abdomen distending as he went into shock. We called the surgeon, and he went to theatre. I was surprised how cross I was that I was missing independence. We had a radio, and I was irritated by those coming in with scabies. I felt they could have waited one more day, after all it was never going to happen again.

I was invited to a couple of social functions that night but didn't go because I was too tired and had nothing to wear. The invitation said informal dress, but that is misleading.

People either turn up in formal dress or fit for a state ball. I will send you both independence issues.[40]

I then continued that I had got dad's letter about taking care after independence and said I was already conscious of it:

I will have to be more cautious. I had an altercation with a man who was a little drunk and rather dogmatic. I was explaining how to care for children with fevers. His wife was very apologetic. It is difficult dealing with an acute emergency and then getting back to less urgent cases. People are usually grateful as I generally move fast (ibid).

Talking to one of my NZ friends, I realised the locals got jealous because the Europeans seemed so wealthy. I felt resentful when I went into the Honiara Butchery and watched the Europeans spending $20 on pork, eggs and ice-cream while I lined up for mince.

George agreed there could be more anti-white feeling after independence but thought the church would be a stabilising influence.

Three weeks later I was transferred to the female ward. A man I had argued with had made a complaint.

The medical superintendent had a complaint from a senior government official about the way I treated his child.

His child had been poked in the eye with a coat hanger and had no obvious injury. It was night and there was no doctor available as they are only on call for emergencies.

I told him to come back in the morning to see the doctor. The medical superintendent said I did the right thing but he was concerned about the racist tone. He said he was very happy with my work (in fact, he said it was outstanding, the first praise I have received). He said however to protect the hospital and me he wanted to move me to a quieter place. He said after independence all countries were inclined to become more nationalistic.

I said I was perfectly happy to go and had been abused by a public servant before. It is interesting it is not the ordinary people who resent me (I get on very well with them) but the top public servants and some politicians. They lead far more comfortable lives than I do.

I am glad mum has now decided on her date. The village has now got a fast canoe donated by an Overseas Aid Programme. All I have to do is send a service message on the radio and the canoe will come and get us.[41]

Chapter 3

MUM'S VISIT, SEDITION, CYCLONES AND PREGNANCY

Mum visited us in the first half of 1978. After a year's absence, my father had got a job in Hong Kong again, but mum was yet to find work as a teacher. We visited the emergency department and then flew to Kirakira and took the canoe to the village, complete with water-seal toilet and fuel for our return voyage.

We waited off Tawatana for a good wave and then shot towards the beach and the gathered crowd. Our gear was handed from hand to hand and we walked up to our hut on the plateau. A mattress was found for mum and the toilet quickly installed in the old coral in the bush out the front.

Mum was well looked after. A small boy followed a chicken until it laid an egg for her breakfast. We toured the school and she and Rebi companionably smoked around the fire unable to speak with each other.

We got the time of our return flight to Honiara wrong and while in the canoe saw the plane flying back to Honiara. It took us to three days to catch the next one and meanwhile we stayed with long-suffering relatives. We ate freshly caught crayfish once, a meal mum fondly remembers as one of the best in her life. Luckily, she did not miss her flight back to Hong Kong.

Mum thoroughly enjoyed the whole experience and wrote a detailed letter to her sister Diana in Waitara, New Zealand, in late August 1978.

> Rebi was bringing up three of her eldest daughter's children. The youngest was three. We spent the morning having a swim. My togs created a stir. People don't swim in the sea although they do go spearfishing in their clothes. When they get out they have a dip in the river, wash their clothes and put them on a rock to dry.
>
> There were lots of visits with lots of hand shaking. Some of the houses had a few shelves of things for sale but there wasn't much. It was a long time since a ship had called, so all their copra had gone bad. There wasn't much money. Somebody produced an egg for my lunch, and it was very nice. Every egg is regarded as a potential chick which is worth a dollar. There were lots of hens, a few pigs and dogs, and one cat. There were also a fair number of flies, but very few mosquitoes.
>
> We went to see the gardens where most people work during the day. They use the land for two years and then shift to another site by chopping down and burning more forest.
>
> The soil is very fertile, volcanic, and the island

underpopulated. The villages are along the coast and there are still vast areas of jungle with large hardwood trees. They grow kumaras (sweet potatoes), two sorts of taro (both ghastly), sweet corn, pineapple, mango, long beans, cassava, pawpaws and tobacco which they roll up in Chinese exercise books and smoke. Many of the older women smoke pipes, are bare-breasted, and some have tattoos. Unfortunately, it was too rough to go fishing. George's father Basil went out with a bow and arrow and tried to shoot a pigeon but was unsuccessful.

We toured the school, about four huts with desks and a blackboard in each. The schoolmaster was very nice and got seven students into the National High School which Margaret said was better than average. Some of the pupils boarded during the week as their villages were a long way away. They fed themselves from their own gardens. He said some of the children were kept at home by their parents especially during planting time, but most of them attended occasionally.

We visited a large garden in another village which belonged to George's mother and was looked after by her brother Haruta. The system of inheritance is matrilineal, but the land is farmed by one person, chosen by the father, ensuring it is not divided. The jungle seems to belong to anyone who is prepared to clear it.

The church is another hut. The people are expected to go twice a day but not many do. The older ones go to a singsong on Saturday nights. Sunday is a rest day and they do not do any gardening.

George's mother was very upset we were not staying longer as they didn't have time to collect our gifts. George got one of the boys to walk to another village about three hours away to get some beer and the men had a small party on Sunday night on the beach.

We left fairly early on Monday morning but because we had to call into another village to get some fuel, we missed the plane. There was another one on Wednesday so we didn't worry, although George was upset because he had a paper to put out. We spent the two days at Kirakira with a friend of Georges who was clerk of the council, a paid mayor of the town. They were very kind to us.

We went down in the morning to see the market. As they are all government servants, they have no gardens and have to buy all their food. It is bought in from outlying villages and there is not enough. There is a terrible scramble, worse than Hong Kong. Among the buyers was the English doctor and his missionary wife from Auckland. The town has a bakery but they ran out of flour earlier in the week. We ate food from an oven like a hangi but the food tasted better, or perhaps I was hungrier.

The houses are like the ones in Honiara and hotter than the leaf huts. We went for a couple of swims rather a long way from town as no-one was sure of the sewerage.

On Wednesday, five of us turned up at the airport in

Chapter 3 Mum's visit, sedition, cyclones and pregnancy

the tractor provided. The plane arrived. It was already full. I had words with the Australian pilot who said he was always on the sharp end of these mix ups! To add insult to injury the tractor disappeared and we had to walk back to town, leaving our luggage which included a hen in a basket someone had given us.

We arrived back to our long-suffering hostess and tried to find out if we would be stuck there forever. Margaret rang the airline in Honiara the following day. We could only ring at certain times, and it was a radio telephone with lots of 'over and outs'. She managed to get our two names on the list but was told they were the only two seats available. This wasn't good as another of the of the stranded passengers had an international flight on Saturday. I rang the head chap and he promised to send a larger plane to get us all out. It was a rather anxious two days but we finally all got on the plane on Friday afternoon.

I went to see the manager, a New Zealander, but didn't have much joy. I got a lecture on the difficulty of running an airline in the Solomons. I suggested they change their agent in Kirakira as we could never find him, but he said that wasn't possible for political reasons.

Apart from the travel difficulties, I really enjoyed the trip and feel reassured about Margaret. There will be political difficulties, particularly in Honiara, but there isn't as much anti-European feeling as in Hong Kong.

In late August I wrote to my parents telling them how much we all enjoyed mum's visit and how important it was for George's family to finally meet her.[42]

As a botany teacher, mum was fascinated by Basil's knowledge about medicinal plants and advised me to gather and document that knowledge during my next visit. Sadly, I never did.

Work in the female ward was very dreary. I made beds and washed people, and got so bored I applied for a job as a women's interest officer for Central Province.

Two weeks later I met John Sisiolo, the chief nursing officer, and told him I was looking for other work. He said they were very short of nursing tutors as the two expatriates' contracts finished at the end of 1979 and only one local was being trained to replace them.[43]

In September 1978 I was nursing a premature baby whose mother had died. This was relatively common as pregnant women referred from the provinces sometimes arrived too late. I was on night duty, dreamily watching the expressed breast milk from another mother going down the baby's tube and wondering whether I should adopt her. It is just as well I didn't because shortly after I found I was pregnant.

It was bizarre that George and I didn't understand why I was nauseous. We were puzzling over it, when Welshman Teilo, George's mentor and father of five, arrived.

'Why, she's pregnant,' he said.

This was confirmed by early October after I had

vomited for two weeks. I lost four kilos and had a longing for sausages, eggs, milk, cheese, apples and fish; all very expensive.

When the chief nursing officer asked me to go to Australia during 1979, I had to decline so he said he would organise a two-year nurse education diploma course from an Australian university. That induced me to stay, so when I was offered the women's interest job I turned it down.

I was working an afternoon shift on 22 October 1978 when I heard a flight to Bellona had not returned. I was haunted by the image of the pilot's wife and their children waiting at the airport. It was the first major tragedy for Solomon Airlines (SolAir) in its ten-year history. It was the same plane mum, George and I flew in from Kirakira.

> The plane carrying eleven passengers and the pilot plunged into the sea after leaving Rennell, one of the outer islands. He left Rennell in bad weather and the fog closed in. He attempted to fly to Honiara but lost his bearings so returned to Rennell. He circled for some time but could see nothing so finally left for Honiara. At 12.45 he radioed in saying he had run out of fuel. That was the last they heard from him.
>
> SolAir planes immediately went to look for them. Australia and the New Hebrides sent a plane each. Yesterday, six planes and two boats were scouring the area, however nothing was found. This country is so small then everyone knows at least one person who died.[44]

An enquiry in late February 1979, found that the Bellona navigational beacon was not working. All flights to the island were suspended until the navigational beacon was repaired.[45]

In that same letter, I spoke of my brief hospital admission:

> I was vomiting and miserable so I decided after reading Margaret Myles (a classic midwifery text) that I had hyperemesis. I went to see Dr Quan, that nice Chinese doctor we saw at Kirakira, mum. He admitted me overnight to the private ward. I had a drip for sixteen hours and three very nice European meals including bacon and eggs. It cost me $10 but it was worth it. With the judicious use of Avomine and regular meals my vomiting has now stopped.

I also spoke of George who was about to appear in court, charged with sedition for printing *The West Wind*:

The case was embarrassing for the government because it raised the question of why the locals who included *The West Wind* in the government paper were not prosecuted.

> The Australian Press Association has called George and said they are interested in the case. And the news will circulate to Fiji PNG et cetera (George is Radio PNG's correspondent).
>
> I am applying to Armidale College to do a nursing

education diploma. It's a two-year correspondence course and recognised in Australia. I am seeing the Australian Aid representative on Monday. The chief nursing officer, Mr Sisiolo, is also organising training for others.

My parents were very happy about our news and I was able to confirm with them after seeing the NZ High Commissioner that from Feb 1978, the baby could claim NZ citizenship. I also told them I had been offered another job by the YWCA as coordinator and was happy to know I had employment choices.[46]

A week later I updated them on George's court case. He was about to go to court to enter a plea of not guilty, with the case to be heard on 8 December. As a precaution, in case he was jailed, George asked an experienced journalist from the provinces to come and work with him.

I was much happier in the female ward as I was now in charge. It was a mixed medical and surgical ward and one of the challenges was preparing the theatre cases. The theatre kept changing their mind about who they wanted next.[47]

A week later I had seen the obstetrician and was worried.

The midwives told me about a woman with a breech delivery left unattended when she was fully dilated and ready to give birth. The baby was born dead.

Another woman due in two weeks found she no longer had foetal movements and the midwife couldn't hear the foetal heart. She was told not to worry. That baby too was born dead.

He refused to admit another pregnant woman with a very high blood pressure who was in danger of fitting. The midwife insisted she was admitted.

I will go over to Malaita just before I am due in mid-May if needed. There is a good obstetrician over there.

I have also met Jane again who has returned to the Solomons with Mackay, the Solomon Islands Nurse. He is making $130 a month and she doesn't have a job. They are paying $100 per month rent, and surviving on $30 a month. They eat taBioca or cassava, tinned fish and bush cabbage. I dug through the freezer and gave her some meat.[48]

Just before Christmas I thanked my parents for the hundred dollars they sent and told them how Jane and I had gone to the Mendana hotel and had pork salad, sandwiches and ice-cream for $5 each. The rest of the money I was saving for baby things and maternity frocks. I continued:

We got a fright when we woke up this morning. My suitcase with my clothes wasn't there. We found it outside with belongings scattered around it.

We called the police who found footprints which showed three men had been watching the house from the bank. One had come in when Jane and I went out briefly that evening. There were two boys sleeping in the house and I didn't lock the door.

They left everything except my purse with $6 in it, my two bankbooks, my passport and your registered article card. I rushed down to the post office and got the $100, stopped my bank accounts and reported my lost passport to the New Zealand High Commission.

George was talking wildly about getting a shotgun and a bow and arrow but he has calmed down now.

We have decided to get a dog to warn us of intruders and lock the house. We will both have keys. I will keep my passport in the bank.[49]

On 3 January 1979, a telegram — George acquitted.

George gave evidence that he received the poem *The West Wind* on May 1978 and put it aside as it was unsigned. During the preparation of the 27 September 1978 edition an advertiser suddenly withdrew two pages and George had difficulty filling the paper. He asked Macpherson Taro, his administrative assistant to continue with the layout and left. Macpherson found the poem and because it was short and fitted the space, put it in.

Macpherson told the court he titled it *Local War* because that seemed appropriate. George said he didn't know the poem had been included until he saw it in the published *Toktok*. George was not convicted as he had not exhibited intent.[50]

At times I felt very far away from my family. This is the letter I wrote after I was told of my paternal grandfather's death:

> I suppose you are back in Hong Kong now dad. I was very upset to hear about Grandpa's death. It was very unexpected. I knew from the letter that Pete wrote and Mum forwarded that he was disorientated but I didn't expect him to die.
>
> You say he died, as he lived, with courage and dignity. Ever since I have been old enough to understand I have appreciated his integrity and courage. He is one of the best of us and has been an example to us all. I was very happy to hear he died peacefully, with some of his family around him and was buried in a way fitting to his life. It is on such occasions I feel how deeply my loyalties are divided. I was very sorry not to be with the family on such an occasion, just as I was very sorry to miss Pete (my brother) and Wendy's wedding.
>
> However, I think Grandpa would appreciate how we are blown all over the world. He would understand, because he was a man who never flinched, either from life or death.[51]

In February, I was finally teaching and surprised that, although the students were form five graduates, they knew little about basic functions such as the working of the heart or breathing. I wrote the vital notes on the board but the students couldn't take them down. I was worried they would have nothing to revise with. Sister Hayes, the tutor, told me not to worry and said they got faster at writing.

The new curriculum was also a worry. After six months, the students would not be able to do anything but take temperatures. This was Central Hospital where I had been confronted by a doctor a couple of days earlier because a junior student nurse hadn't coped well when a baby with neonatal tetanus had a cardiac arrest and died. The doctor said the tetanus was mild. I couldn't understand why a nursing student was looking after that baby alone. Meanwhile, George was in court again:

> George was back in court last week. He was sued for $10,000 by Mr Kinika, the Deputy Prime Minister, about a poem which was published in April last year.
>
> Happily, the settlement ended up with George just paying him $374 which means the paper wasn't ruined. George has been more careful recently.
>
> We have been going to a lot of cocktail parties recently. You meet the same people, drunken politicians and occasionally nice people. Two ministers embarrassed me.
>
> One asked me when I would get pregnant, when I clearly was, and the other asked me to teach his eleven-year-old son English for an hour a day. As though I haven't got anything else to do.[52]

In the middle of February in 1979, there was a big cyclone in Makira which blew down most of the huts in Tawatana.

Peter Adams, George's brother, arrived in Honiara with $200 worth of copra and sold it for $300. He said it would be the last copra for a while as many coconut trees were blown down and the nuts twisted on others.

He said he was so busy helping others he forgot the $400 he had left in his store which blew down. His house blew down too but luckily no-one was inside. I continued:

> They used the leaf that was still good to make smaller houses. They still have kumaras but these will run out soon as the gardens were uprooted. It will be six months before new kumaras are ready.
>
> It will be five years before the trees they make houses with will grow back. A relief committee has been formed to collect money for food. The government and other countries are helping. The people will live on tinned fish and rice for a while.
>
> George is going back to the village. This cyclone has shaken everyone's confidence. There have been a lot more cyclones in the past twenty years.
>
> It's hard to plan when you don't know when everything is going to be blown down.[53]

In early March, George toured the affected areas with the Prime Minister, Peter Kenilorea, and took four bags of rice and eight tins of biscuits with him. Meanwhile, Welshman

Chapter 3 Mum's visit, sedition, cyclones and pregnancy

Teilo looked after the newspaper and I went in to check the letters. I was also very happy the excellent obstetrician Dr Maemaruki from Malaita was back in Honiara. He confirmed all was well. I continued:

> Jane just reminded me the baby will need a name. Could you please send one of those small books of common names from Hong Kong. The baby will need a custom name too, but George can think of that. I'm looking forward to seeing George again. He should be back next week.[54]

Finally George returned.

> The hills and mountains in the Arosi One district have turned brown because the trees have lost their foliage. They look like dead dry reeds. No green can be seen except along the shoreline where some coconuts are still standing. There are a few gardens which are still green, with smoke rising from fires there. People are slowly recovering and replanting.
>
> The sea between Makira and Ugi was brown with floating mud and logs. Mudslides damaged Aringana Clinic and Toroi School.
>
> Bauro district experienced heavy seas which swept a hundred yards inland, sweeping away houses, animals and uprooting trees.
>
> Kirakira waterfront looked like an abandoned quarry

with dead coral, gravel and stone swept thirty yards into the station. Kapok trees were down, and the airport, roads and bridges damaged.

The party also toured Ugi Island where Pawa Secondary School had been hit. One student said during the cyclone, comma corrugated iron was blown around like pots. School has been postponed while new dormitories are built.[55]

George said the cyclone sounded terrifying, with darkness in the middle of the day, houses collapsing, and rain so hard it bruised the skin. The European female doctor on tour was crying all the time.

Tawatana is now very hot because all the leaves have been blown off the trees. Eighty per cent of the coconut trees were blown down, and people are rebuilding their houses and some are already replanting coconuts and gardens. During George's absence the paper lost money, but we should be all right with my salary. Someone who hadn't seen me for a while saw my face at the supermarket and said, 'You're getting thinner', then she laughed when the rest of me emerged.[56]

We were shocked when Colin, the author of *The West Wind*, was jailed for three months. We gave his family food, and later his wife Namoi came and looked after Brian.

After a week of scrubbing the house and buying baby

things I went to stay with Father Abel and his wife Agnes at Selwyn College, thirty minutes' drive south of Honiara.

> Agnes is six months pregnant too, but with her ninth child. She has five of the children back from Tawatana as the school there had blown down. I was asked to teach First Aid and did so.
> After seeing two piles of faeces on the way to the river I thought I would be better occupied teaching hygiene and sanitation. The house is empty while I am writing except for one small boy and myself. Everyone else is at church. They are tolerant of my disinclination to attend church every evening, and as for George they regard him as a pagan.[57]

In my next letter a week later I wrote about the children:

> I am really enjoying the five children who range from four up to thirteen. They haven't got any toys so they make them. The four-year-old carves little dolls out of bark and plays with them in the dirt. The eight-year-old has made a game of snakes and ladders including the dice. The thirteen-year-old has made a treehouse, well a tree platform. They all play with a ball their mother has made them which is stuffed with their father's hair! All the packets and old tins are carefully collected, assessed and kept.[58]

A couple of weeks before I was due we had another burglary.

A couple of nights ago, thieves lifted the louvres out in the kitchen and came through while we were sleeping. They stole George's big radio cassette recorder, a kettle, a pot and a few glasses. I woke in the morning with the dog licking my feet. There are usually two doors between us and him.

George went to the police for insurance purposes. That day we put thick wire netting over the kitchen louvres. We have been locking the outside door and now we are locking our bedroom door. The dogs usually bark but they must have thrown them some meat.

There are many burglaries in Honiara. The New Zealander a couple of doors down has recently been burgled twice.

On the other hand, I enjoyed having six people from the village stay with us the other night. They buy their own food, cook for themselves and clean up afterwards and we catch up with their news. Some people's gardens are producing kumara again. Peter Adams is still buying copra (I don't know where from) and his working capital has increased from $200 to $400.[59]

As delivery grew closer, I hoped I would not be called upon to give up my baby if I had a girl and Agnes had a boy. She had eight sons and wanted this last child to be a girl. Happily, Agnes gave birth to Abeline, named after her father, while I had Brian.

Chapter 4

BRIAN'S BIRTH, SCHOOL OF NURSING

Two days after Brian was born on 18 May 1979 I wrote to my parents. George had sent them a telegram immediately after the birth.

> I started having mild contractions around 10.30 am on the 18th and went to the antenatal clinic. The doctor did a vaginal examination and found I was 3 cm dilated, so I still had a further 7 cm to go. He ruptured my membranes and sent me to hospital. I saw the Scottish obstetrician around 3pm. He looked at me approvingly and told me to keep walking around. At 5 pm, I started having quite strong contractions. George and my friend and colleague Avira from the School of Nursing appeared and said they were going to have tea. George said they wouldn't be back until 7.30pm. I told them I would have had the baby by then.
>
> Towards the end, I found the contractions unbearable. They gave me pethidine and 15 minutes later I vomited. I

yelled I was going to push and the sister who was outside rushed in. In two pushes the baby's head was out, and in the next push the baby. There was a mild panic as nothing was ready. They didn't have time to do an episiotomy and I got a vaginal wall tear as I pushed the baby out. As they stitched it up, I decided that was more painful than giving birth. George and Avira then returned.

The baby is big but not fat. (He was 3.5 kg). I am surprised how much harder it is to look after your own baby than nurse other people's, still my sore perineum and afterpains don't help. He is breastfeeding well but needs extra bottles.

I am grateful I have my own room in the private ward. It's a homely building away from the hospital with a lovely veranda, surrounded by trees, and cool sea breezes.

I was going to go to the public ward but the sister said the private ward was free to hospital staff (a new regulation). Not only is there privacy but good food. Perhaps I deserve it because I look after myself. I check my fundus, to feel my uterus is contracting and shrinking, take my salt baths three times a day and check the baby's temperature.

I am trying hard to avoid infection. Everything is so different from NZ. Even the delivery packs aren't sterilised. They just soak the instruments. I use toilet paper for everything, from cleaning my breasts, to cleaning the baby's bottom. So perhaps just getting sticky eyes isn't so bad.

We have called the baby Brian. We will send a photo when he looks a bit better.⁶⁰

Two days later, I wrote:

There is no need for postnatal exercises when you are in a place like this. I washed 15 nappies this morning.

Everyone was very impressed with the quick delivery. Dr Maemaruki said it was because I was so fit. He also checked the baby over thoroughly and said he was healthy. He will discharge me in a couple of days. Perhaps it's just as well. I'm getting quite involved with nursing the other patients..⁶¹

A week later, I wrote again. Brian had developed an infection:

The baby developed thrush and blisters around his scrotum. I went down to the hospital, couldn't find a doctor, was given Nystatin for the thrush and came home.

Today I discovered the blisters have turned to pus so I returned to the hospital.

I met the physician, had a cup of coffee with him, and told him I was worried.

He checked the baby and prescribed intramuscular Crystapen 25,000 units daily which I give him with disposable syringes. I am also painting his scrotal blisters with gentian violet, applying hibitane after his bath, and boiling his nappies. The doctor will check him again next Tuesday or earlier if I am worried. He seems fine now, calm, no temperature and he's feeding well.

I too am much better, my stitches have healed and I don't feel so tired. I was hoping to go out to Selwyn College tomorrow for my birthday but we won't now.[62]

At the end of July I was back at work and enjoying it. The physician asked the patients what they would they do if they had a million dollars to spend on their districts. Perhaps of more relevance was the large number of TB cases we noted, particularly TB of the bone. Liver cirrhosis due to drinking was also relatively common, as was lung cancer due to smoking. Kidney disease, particularly the nephrotic syndrome, was also widespread. The physician thought it may have been due to custom medicine. Later I decided it was probably due to infection by Streptococcus B, as there was also a lot of rheumatic heart disease.

I also wrote about a boat that had sunk a couple of weeks earlier. A radio broadcast had asked the public to look for the crew. A taxi driver had described it to me as 'rusty underneath' and George's article in the *Toktok* confirmed this.

> The *Sisco* sank between Santa Cruze and Santa Anna in the Eastern Solomons on Friday, and was captained by its Australian owner, Paul Burges. On Thursday night, an engineer noticed seawater coming through the bow.

The hole was patched with cement but began to give way the next morning. Later that morning water began flooding into the cabins. An order was given to leave the ship and a May Day message radioed to Honiara just after midday on Friday.

The fifteen men on board drifted in a lifeboat for fifty-three hours. They sighted Santa Anna on Saturday evening when they were twenty miles away. They had two Yamaha engines and plenty of food and fresh water.

An intensive air search began with two SolAir aircraft and one from NZ. They failed to spot the men because of poor visibility. The lifeboat was seen by the *Orion*, from the Royal Australian Navy on Sunday and was picked up by the Tulagi. The marine division of the Ministry of Transport and Communications is carrying out an inquiry.[63]

In August I wanted to go to Malaita with Brian to visit the third-year nursing students, but George stopped it. He told me about a group of villagers, who after covering themselves with mud, threatened neighbouring villagers with shotguns.

We had the Minister of Education for a meal. He was very interested in a relative's father who claimed he had taught children to read and write in three weeks. We were told that after this he almost had a mental breakdown.[64]

I remember waiting with Barnabas (George's uncle) and Eunice while their five-year-old daughter Alison underwent open heart surgery. It was successful and was the first open heart surgery performed by a visiting Australian cardiac surgical team in the Solomons. Ali was transformed from a sickly toddler into a healthy child and went on to marry, have her own children and become the head teacher at Tawatana School.[65]

In August, George was elected to the Honiara town council and in September became vice-mayor. They began a radio anti-litter campaign, lobbied to get a big oil installation in the middle of town moved, advocated for pedestrian crossings opposite the hospital and the market, a footpath in Vura, picnic areas at a town beach, and the removal of a hotel from a residential area.

The doctors' dispute continued. Instead of reaching a settlement with the local doctors, the Ministry of Health recruited more expatriates. In October 1979, an Australian locum surgeon, posted for three months, caused concern.

> The postoperative infection rate has increased, he offends the local staff, and a European woman who had a hysterectomy has now got a paralytic ileus (her large intestine no longer works). Meanwhile the government has not met the local doctors' demands for an increase in salary and they are beginning to resign.
>
> We had a very capable surgical intern who could have done the surgeon's job for three months but he has now resigned.[66]

In November 1979 two new tutors were appointed, one from England whom I described as a tough, experienced woman who believed in objectives, teaching methods and evaluation.

She didn't like the current syllabus where hookworm was mixed up with breech delivery and wanted obstetrics separated out. She described the new curriculum as jargon and impossible to teach. The doctors agreed with her.[67]

In December I was both a tutor and charge nurse. During one week, as well as managing the female ward, I had seven hours of lectures, one afternoon shift in charge of the hospital and I marked fourteen final medical papers, completed an assignment for Armidale and looked after Brian. At least I was not alone in this. Basil, who was staying with us, also took care of him, speaking to him in Arosi.

I enjoyed the ward. I had good nurses and got on well with the doctors. I wrote:

> The physician had me tapping a woman's chest and looking at her X-rays the other day. As a tutor, he feels I should know a bit more.[68]

We had a good Christmas that year, visiting George's Uncle Barnabas, Eunice and Ali over at Taroniara for four days. Barnabas was in charge of the Anglican shipbuilding and repair business and they had a big house on a peninsula surrounded by the sea. There was a little church and a small hospital with three nurses.

It was half an hour by boat from Tulagi, the previous capital of the Solomons. We were paddled out to two sunken ships, an American cargo boat and a Japanese warship. It was very moving to see these great hulks among the mangroves and bays and gave new meaning to its name, Iron Bottom Sound.

We also visited an Indian who lived on a small island:

> It is the most beautiful island I have seen with white sand and very clear water, straight out of a tourist brochure. He has started a boat building business there. The locals who work for him lived in nice houses and as he has the only shop on the island, he retrieves about a third of their salaries by selling them beer.
>
> He is married to a local woman and they have six children. He has built himself a $18,000 house on the highest point of the island with all mod cons. We walked up there and drank cold Fanta and beer while looking over the view.
>
> I was sorry to come back and went straight to the hospital to a busy afternoon shift. We had two deaths, a possible fractured spine and a man with a cut jugular who needed an emergency tracheostomy. I admitted a woman with dysentery.[69]

In the next letter, I complained how difficult we found

it looking after mental health patients in a general ward particularly this woman with schizophrenia.

> She wanders off, and once took her clothes off and lay down in the middle of the road. Some nights she keeps everyone awake banging and shouting.
> She has dismantled her room and defecated in it. There is a specialist mental health ward in Malaita but the doctor doesn't want to send her there.[70]

In early February, I invited the senior nursing tutor home to tea. Unfortunately, that night we ate a pig's head, the first and only time we ever ate it.

> There is not much meat on it. It was the worst meal we have had for months. After I had finished apologising, we went to the movies at the Guadalcanal (G) Club. There was the head of school, me, Ida and the other girl living here. This was despite George's protests. He thinks the G Club is a den of inequity.[71]

It was hectic, especially if Brian was sick. I described a day when I had to cope with Brian, who had a fever, the ward, and tutoring:

> On Friday 24 February 1980 I rushed down to work at 6.45 am with Brian and Ida, went to the ward, allocated the staff, got Brian sorted with Malaria Blood slide

et cetera. At 7.30 I went to the school, did two hours' teaching, then went back to Brian and Ida, got his prescription for antimalarials then sent them home.

Back at the ward I found a case of meningococcal meningitis had been admitted, involving full barrier nursing with special nurses. Every contact had to be given a sulfadimidine course. Then we had a blood transfusion that afternoon and a bone marrow puncture. In between times I went back to the school, taught for half an hour and gave them another project to do.[72]

There was a much more relaxed day on Sunday when we went out to Selwyn College. After church I chatted with Father Abel.

He told me about the Europeans who lived around Tawatana a hundred years ago.

Some were deserters from ships, and some were convicts from Australia who weren't in a hurry to go back to England. The local chiefs adopted some of them, and some of them would even go and fight. There is cave near Tawatana where you can see a sailing ship carved in the stone.[73]

It was only March and I was already ordering my birthday presents for early June:

If you are thinking of getting me a birthday present you

might consider a watch. I need one with a second hand. The watch you had mended, Mum, has fallen to pieces and the watch George bought me doesn't have a second hand. I can't take pulses. It's a problem for a nurse.

Another trial has been the lack of water over the past three days. The only time it came on was 2 am. I left the tap on and when I heard it running I would leap up, fill every available container in the house and have a shower. Rather exhausting at that time of the morning. Happily we have water back on now.

We recently had a phone installed. It is fascinating. You can't dial out most of the time. If it is ringing and you pick it up you can hear the other person talking but they can't hear you.

We saw the World Health Organisation woman on Monday. She has decided she will send us to Papua New Guinea after Australia in August.

The head of school offered to send me to Tulagi for a few days to teach their village health aids but George wouldn't let me go.[74]

The government decided the Honiara town council was misusing money and threatened to dissolve it. However, the Auditor General disagreed:

> He said the financial management in the town council is much better than most of the provinces. Apparently dissolving the town council would be unconstitutional so

they will amend the Constitution. George said the council may take the matter to the High Court.^(ibid)

By the end of March 1980 the local doctors' call for a salary increase was still dragging on.

> The local doctors are still working to rule after eighteen months and the expatriate doctors are now beginning to refuse to undertake any after-hours work except emergency surgery. Meanwhile the MPs have voted themselves $4000 redundancy pay each.[75]

The public and workers were incensed about the MPs' proposed redundancy pay and a month later George was due to attend a meeting with all the unions to discuss a strategy. He was also preparing to write about some of the decisions by the Ministry of Health and Medical Services.

> Next week George is going to expose an expatriate who is being funded by the government to fly to Australia for a hernia repair. It could have been done here. However, they refused to pay the fares for a local man to access lifesaving treatment in Australia. Instead, the Lions are funding the fare.
> The government is now hastily trying to recruit more overseas doctors as the local doctors continue to resign. It would be cheaper and more sustainable to increase their wages.[76]

On Thursday 1 May 1980, the Public Service Association held a march demanding the government solve the dispute with the local doctors. Two thousand people marched. I wasn't among them.

On Friday the doctors met with the government again and there was hope a settlement will be reached.[77]

In July and early August, I was in Australia with five other nursing tutors at Armidale College. On our way back, we spent two weeks in Papua New Guinea. I include a letter about the Highlands, written in mid-August, which I had often discussed with Solomon Islands nurses who trained up there. It was good to finally see it for myself:

> I'm writing from Mt Hagen in the Western Highlands. We have been here two days and fly back to Port Moresby this afternoon, then back to the Solomons tomorrow.
>
> When we arrived we were driven out to the hospitals and aid posts. It is a fascinating if sombre place. It is a vast country, rains a lot, always has lowering clouds and is very fertile. It is incredible Europeans have only been up here for the past fifteen to twenty years.
>
> It is quite densely populated with bush gardens and clearings over the smaller hills. The scattered huts are low, with grass roofs and woven walls, no windows and a dirt floor. They are grouped in hamlets.
>
> There were a lot of people wandering around, most of the men without trousers, a cloth in front and grass behind. There was a lady walking along the road with a

small pig on a lead. Apparently, they even suckle them, a baby on one breast, a piglet on the other.

There are a lot of tea plantations owned by expatriates, and coffee plantations owned by locals. Some of the villagers also grow coffee and sell it to passing trucks.

There is not a lot of tribal fighting at present. It usually occurs because of payback. If one member of my tribe is harmed or robbed, then I have the right to payback. It is complicated by sickness and perceived sorcery. Sometimes when the nursing students return to their villages, they need to be heavily guarded.

Mt Hagen itself is small, with about 4000 people, but thriving with little shops and Chinese stores. The main health problems are chest infections, excluding TB. There was a lot of leprosy but there is less now. There is an increase in malaria which has come up from the coast, a lot of venereal disease and some malnutrition. Pigbel is very common here. People feast on pork and there is massive increase in their gut of a certain bacteria. This can cause obstruction, so the gut can burst causing peritonitis. They now have a vaccine. The nurses run the clinics as in the Solomons.[78]

It was so sad when a child the same age as Brian died suddenly from meningitis in October 1980. I knew the family and found it so distressing I couldn't attend his funeral.

> This has been a very sad day. I have just learnt about an eighteen-month-old who died on Wednesday. I know the mother and father, very nice Australians. The child was lively and healthy. On Wednesday morning, he had a fever and his mother tepid sponged him, thinking it was the flu. He played all day, and in the evening had a convulsion.
>
> They took him straight to the hospital where the doctor did a lumbar puncture. While the doctor went to check the results the child had another convulsion and died. He could not be resuscitated and was diagnosed with haemophilus meningitis. All his contacts are being treated with a course of antibiotics. This death has really shaken us up. You realise how precarious life is. He was the couple's only child.
>
> I have also learnt today that the government cannot give me a permanent job. They say if they can replace me with a local, they will. This may be difficult, for even if we all qualify, we will be short of tutors.[79]

That Christmas, George and I and Brian spent in New Zealand with my family. It was so good to have a break from the Solomons. But reality struck quickly when we returned, as my letter written in April 1981 reflected:

> The three relatives staying here all disappeared this week leaving no-one to look after Brian. A boy who used to work here is coming back in a couple of days and meanwhile I'm doing all the washing and cleaning.

Brian went to a relative's house on Friday and seemed very happy there. While mummy and daddy are around, he doesn't seem to mind which relatives come and go.

On Friday I arranged for the WHO expert on malaria to come and answer our questions. Malaria is beginning to get out of control. The dangerous type, falciparum, is widespread and the parasite has developed chloroquine resistance.

George seems to have recovered from his bout of malaria. Meanwhile I am taking chloroquine prophylactically because I am pregnant and both myself and the foetus are at higher risk.[80]

Chapter 5

PREGNANCY, JOHN'S BIRTH AND LEAVING NURSING

At last, in April 1981, I found a reliable carer for Brian, Namoi, Colin's wife.

> Namoi said Brian copies everything she does and tries to help. It can be trying, but we encourage it. Next week she will bring some children for Brian to play with.[81]

A week after a boat trip with Brian to Taroniara at Easter, I got sick.

> I'm at home on sick leave for fourteen days. Three days ago my urine turned bright yellow and I went to the doctor who confirmed I have hepatitis A. It is endemic here. I'm convinced I got it from the filthy lavatory on the ship. I have lost my appetite and vomit in the evenings. My pupils are slightly yellow and I have no liver pain although my liver is slightly enlarged. The doctor said there was no danger to the baby.

> I brought back a dose of gamma globulin to give to George. A bout of hepatitis on top of his malaria would be too much. Brian will have to take his chances. I am studying and preparing lessons.[82]

By mid-May, I was back at work. I found the head of school was involved in a hospital inquiry about the death of a patient with unstable diabetes. He had been in hospital for two weeks and one morning got the symptoms of hypoglycemia or low blood sugar. The nurses called a doctor but no-one came. He died that evening.

The head of school felt targeted during this enquiry but was able to rebut the allegations made. She was upset, and as a friend and colleague I shared this. I wrote that I felt part of my life was coming to an end.

> The Permanent Secretary must have sensed it because he came over and asked if I wanted another contract. I said I would be happy to accept another year from December 1981 to 1982 and the head of school was happy about this.[83]

At the same time George was enjoying his career. In mid-June he was asked to write a story for the *Far East Asian Economic Review* about Burns Philp's plans to move to the Solomons. The following week he was to go on tour with the Prime Minister to the Russell Islands. I continued:

He has been standing near the phone muttering 'I can't stand it,' for the past five minutes. He finally rang up the radio announcer and corrected him. He advised him not to pronounce Mr Begin as in 'start'. He gets a very cool reception from the Solomon Islands Broadcasting Service as he is always ringing them up.

We were embarrassed too by the government trade official in Japan who was negotiating with Taiyo over fishing rights. He proudly announced on national news that as part of the deal he was given fifty baseball bats and a hundred gloves.

The Australian eye team is back and much to my embarrassment its boss, Dr Galbraith, greeted me with great warmth. He regards me as a survivor, one of the last European nurses left. I was there to organise George's glasses. His current ones have got a large crack in them. They insist however he goes to theatre and gets his eyes examined first. His sight has deteriorated. He often thinks flies and spots on the wall are mosquitoes.[84]

George was away and three days later I wrote to my parents again:

> I have just come back from a very enjoyable evening with Namoi and her family. It was lovely watching the sun setting over the sea. Brian played on some canoes, and we had a lovely meal.

I took rice and yams and there was one plate of chicken which was placed in front of Brian and I. Namoi's husband is in hospital with diabetes.[85]

Later, Colin died and I remember Brian and I going down to the fishing village and Brian staring at his body which, following custom, was laid out so family and friends could say goodbye. I wondered briefly if this was going to cause him problems, but it didn't appear to.

A week later in late June 1981 with many relatives in the house, money short and George still away, I became depressed. I told my parents I didn't know whether it was because of the pregnancy, impending examinations for Armidale or because I was working very hard:

> Mostyn Habu came up to the house yesterday. He said everything is very politicised in the districts, with everyone wanting to be a big man. Jane, who has been living in Kirakira, confirmed this. She said one of the candidates for the national election promised Makira an international airport.[86]

A month later I was more relaxed and had enjoyed a day with the post basic midwifery students.

> We visited the Red Cross Handicapped Centre. There were two partially deaf children, their deafness caused by meningitis. There was also a sad looking three-year-old.

She was fine apart from knock knees and a strange gait. They can't treat her here and nobody can find the money to send her overseas.[87]

I finally went on maternity leave in late August 1981 and Brian and I took the opportunity to visit Barnabas and Eunice in Taroniara. This time we were accompanied by a neighbour and friend, Sue, an English volunteer.

Sue was interviewing local women and taking their photos for a book, *Mi Mere*, or *I am woman* in pidgin. I later reviewed this book when I became a journalist.

I visited the senior nurse at the Tulagi clinic this morning and gave him an obstetrics procedure manual. He has two registered nurse clinics on the two largest islands. There is a population of more than 5000 people and most of those are cared for by village health aides with three months' training. The standard of rural health services will not improve until there are more nurses. That's why we are planning a two-year assistant nurse course.[88]

A week later I wrote:

A woman presented at the clinic here, after she had a seizure one week after delivery and was sent to Honiara. It may have been malaria. She had had a tetanus shot and had no pre-eclampsia antenatally.

Yesterday we left Brian with Eunice, and Sue and I took a canoe to another island where Sue interviewed a village woman. The woman was hardworking and determined to stay in the village and look after her children, pigs and garden. Her husband works as a clerk in Tulagi, an hour away by canoe.

We went to another village to interview a woman involved with youth activities, and then went to a Church Training Centre. Villagers spend a year there learning cooking and sewing. It looked rundown. I left a donation.

Solomon Mamaloni is now Prime Minister and has named his cabinet. His finance minister was founder of the National Workers Union and a very bright man, as is the Minister for Foreign Affairs.

Mamaloni seems determined about provincial development and has appointed a minister for each province to link with the provincial government.

We are going back tomorrow. Brian and I have really enjoyed ourselves. I have learnt about sewing trousers, making baskets and local pudding while Brian enjoyed swimming and playing with local children.[89]

Back in Honiara in early October I looked after George who had malaria again, while Brian and I slept under a mosquito net.

I enjoyed time with Brian and thanked mum for the children's books she had sent, especially the one about

Chapter 5 Pregnancy, John's birth and leaving nursing

crocodiles. I reported Brian and I used to visit a crocodile up the road until it starved to death. This time I had decided on a name for the baby. If it was a boy, I was going to call him John, if a girl Sarah.[90]

I wrote to them about the birth on 26 October, ten days after John's birth:

> I hope you got the telex George sent. It is a boy delivered at 3.30 pm on 16 October. I enjoyed the labour. I took it very calmly doing my breathing exercises and chatting to the nurses. At 1.30 pm they said I was only 4 cm so the doctor sent me for a walk. I went to see the head of school and chatted until about quarter to three and walked back and had the baby!
>
> They told me I wouldn't have it until 9 or 10 at night. This birth was very quick just like Brian's. The baby is fine and so am I. I didn't get any tears although I do have some bad afterpains.
>
> Brian is very good. He carries his teddy around with him everywhere and has even washed it. I think I'll have to get him a washable doll.
>
> George is more optimistic. He went to see the new Prime Minister (his cousin Solomon Mamaloni). He said he would help although we don't know what form that help will take.[91]

On 1 November, I wrote:

Yesterday George was up in the bush for the opening of a gold mine. There has always been gold in that area and now they want to mine it. He said the village nearby was fascinating with the women wearing grass skirts and the men just a loin cloth. Their houses are built on the ground and have very few windows. He bought back some hunks of half raw pork. Even after cooking it for two hours I didn't want to eat it.[92]

On 12 November, three weeks before I was due to resume work, I learnt that I had a job to go back to. The head of school came up at lunchtime and told me I had been given one year's contract on Level 6, the same level as the other tutors.

She was accompanied by a NZ volunteer who had been in Malaita training the third years. She had been sleeping with a bush knife for the past two months as people tried to get into her house.[93]

With a week to go before my maternity leave ended, I was finding the pace of caring for two small children hectic and said I was looking forward to going back to work. I also accompanied Brian on playdates, something I was unused to.

> I will see how much of this letter I can get written before the baby wakes up. He's difficult. I get him settled, race around doing as much housework as possible, and when I am utterly exhausted, he wakes up again.

At two-and-a-half, Brian is very agile. The house-girl and I are constantly modifying the fence which he can climb over in places. He also climbs on to the kitchen roof, although that has been stopped with a few judiciously placed boards.

I also took the children to a mother and babies gathering of Europeans. Brian steadfastly refused to play with the other children. His little local playmate who accompanied us was completely overwhelmed and went to sleep in a corner.[94]

I went back to work, got bronchitis and managed to infect both Brian and the baby. We all took antibiotics.

In mid-December there was a debate about the parliament banning DDT. This led to experts forecasting there could be up to 160,000 cases of malaria annually in a population of 200,000.[95]

In early January 1982, the head of school left and I learnt from the acting chief nursing officer, Margaret L, that the post basic midwifery course was to be stopped. I understood it was the role of the Nurses and Midwives Board to take that decision. The obstetrics tutor and I submitted a report to the board recommending it continue.

Brian was looking forward to going back to kindy after the Christmas break. He was going to turn three mid-year and I was already worrying about which school we would send him to. I was hesitant to send him to a local school as children didn't start until they were seven. I advised my parents the two private schools were very difficult to get into.

> Woodford is very expensive, and for expatriate children, while the Chinese school has 200 applicants for 40 places and the children learn by rote. You can often hear them chanting numbers and words as you go past.[96].

Three days later George and I were listening to a tribute to a well-known political figure who had died.

His grandfather had been captured as a baby during hostilities with another tribe. As was the custom in those days in Makira and some other provinces, he was tossed down the line from person to person.

If the child did not cry, he was allowed to live as a slave. If he did, he was killed. Because he cried, he was put into the grave with his dead mother and was about to be buried alive. However, a woman jumped in, pulled him out and raised him.[97]

George went to Hawaii for a political seminar and I was very glad when he returned in mid-February. I found it challenging, working, caring for the children, and doing the shopping and cooking.[98]

I resigned from my nursing contract on 15 March, giving the hospital one month's notice. I felt comfortable about the move financially, although the paper had not been published for a couple of weeks. Our intention was

Chapter 5 Pregnancy, John's birth and leaving nursing

that I would join George and look after the advertising and accounts.

Meanwhile I was struggling with household matters:

> They have five isolated cases of typhoid in Honiara and everyone is hoping it doesn't spread. We continue to boil water and they have refused to give out vaccinations. Two hospital laboratory workers have it. The water supply is on and off again and we have been told it has E Coli in it.
>
> It is Sunday and a rather sad day. One of my close friends has just left the Solomons, the water has been on and off all day and now I am finally washing by hand at 8pm in case the water goes off again. I had a call from the hospital to say one of the tutor's children was sick and asking me to take two lessons. It is now 9.30 pm and the children have just gone to sleep.[99]

A week later I was more cheerful as George talked about the possibility of Japanese aid. He was also considering starting a cleaning business.

Measles had surfaced in Malaita and Honiara and the doctors were considering having a measles vaccine campaign. They were concerned unvaccinated vulnerable children, weakened by malaria and malnutrition could die.

In March I also wrote:

> There has been a big disturbance in the Western Solomons. People who resent the presence of a timber

company have destroyed $600,000 of housing and $300,000 of equipment. They didn't target the expatriate houses, but those of the locals.[100]

This was the incident which led to the establishment of a new logging act which allowed custom landowners to get logging licences. I wrote about this as a journalist.

In late March a cyclone damaged some parts of the Solomons while Honiara was at the very edge of it. I said the disaster centre established centrally and in the affected provinces, was a big improvement on previous years. There was co-ordination, the police worked hard and the SIBC broadcast 24-hour information.

> There was talk of evacuating the hospital, which is by the sea. I walked down yesterday in big winds, keeping away from the trees. The sea was very high and rough. I talked to the doctors who felt evacuation would not be necessary. However, we were on standby overnight.
>
> This morning George and I went to see the accountant. George has a $450 monthly contract to clean the service areas of the new five-storey office building. He got a $200 advance. We bought some cleaning equipment and have hired three people. I will be responsible for running this business. I feel some guilt about giving up nursing. I have the experience and qualifications in nurse education in a country which is desperately short of nurses, however I

feel I have been driven away. I confirmed with the chief nursing officer recently that I was resigning.

Various senior district nursing officers were muttering about me coming and working with them. Even George was overawed by the response and asked me to think about it. I feel it is the right time to leave now and try something else. The *News Drum* will be stopping at the end of the month and a new group taking over. We need to break through.[101]

In mid-April, after I had left nursing, I worked hard trying to sort out George's finances. That was difficult and I telegrammed my parents, following up with a letter:

You are probably wondering about the telegram. The Provincial Press had told George that he owes them $1300 and they will not print the paper until he has paid it. George has no reserves and cannot make money unless he goes into print so the only option is to ask you for a loan and pay you back slowly. The printing press has been taken away and so he has no outstanding debt there.

I did a few minutes' work for him a week ago and found him a new office with a phone for $100 a month. The present office is $375 a month and has no phone. There is no possibility of us moving into the building yet but I will speak to the accountant when I get back. I also spoke to him about the house the company rents for its workers and he agreed to reorganise it so the company pays $50 of the rent instead of $120.

I had my last day of work yesterday. I am worried about finishing but I think it is the only chance for the business to get on its feet and it is the right time to try it. The people at the hospital have said I can go back if I want to.

It's Friday today and we are booked on the boat on Tuesday night. It's just as well I am going. I am very tired and overwrought. We should be coming back about 15 May.[102]

Chapter 6

JOURNALISM CADET

This was a letter I didn't discover until forty years later among dad's possessions labelled 'Solomons letters'. It was a plea for help from George written on 6 May 1982:

> Dear Ray
>
> I am writing to inform you how things are at present.
>
> Margaret and the family are in the village. They should return next week but I will extend their stay as the business is not going well. There is no money because the paper has not been printed for three months. We paid off the $1300 debt but the printers also wanted the bill of $600 settled for the last issue.
>
> We have moved into the cheaper office but I am the only one here. Most of the staff have left to find other jobs. My two reporters still support us but have not been turning up to work.
>
> I have asked the banks for support but none can help. I feel guilty that I got Margaret to resign from her job, but I really needed her help and I still do. I am sure we have

made the right move and if we can get out this situation we should make better progress.

I have been thinking of getting a job so Margaret and the two reporters could have a go with the paper but I do not think the newsmen could cope without me.

The office cleaning business looks promising.

Finally if you can assist please help before the family arrives from the village. If you are unable to help send a telex so that I can send a message home asking them to stay.

Yours sincerely George Atkin.[103]

I was enjoying the village with my children and a helper, although I wrote to my parents on 15 May that it was a very different experience with children. There was a constant struggle to bath, wash, clothe, feed, water and toilet the children. It was particularly difficult with John as there was nowhere to put him down. He was carried the whole time as local children are. Brian consumed huge quantities of food, followed George's father Basil constantly, and began to 'hear' the language.

During our stay I was called on to look at sick people. I grew very anxious about one child who I thought might have had meningitis. The little girl had a stiff neck, a positive Kernig's sign and a high fever. I suggested her parents take her to Kirakira. They promptly invited the healing ministry to pray over her while Basil gave her some custom medicine. The next day she was better.[104]

I briefly went up into the bush and repeated this when we returned later that year over Xmas, and below is a story I wrote for the *Sun*, our monthly magazine:

John Tarorodo was my guide. He grew up in the bush, and his family was the last to come down to the coast. Originally people lived in the bush in small hamlets of two or three families as they were terrified of headhunters. John said they had no more than two children so they could carry a child each when a warning was sounded. We passed a hollow tree which had been used as a drum.

At Ngaribusu, on a hilltop we saw some huge river stones used for an oven, carried there by a giant warrior called Mwaerobwani.

John Taroroda's father had seen the giant's thighbone. It was as long as an ordinary man's leg. Mwaerobwani lived peaceably with the locals but hunted and killed people from other tribes. Afraid to go to the river, he found a spring which offered natural protection with rocks above and behind him. Water dropped from the rock above into a stone basin about the size of a coconut shell.

The giant was finally killed in his own house while sharpening the point of his spear, foolishly pointed towards his chest. His housekeeper sang a lullaby summoning his enemies and advising them to push the spear in. After his death his friends hid his bones so his enemies could not eat them, and so dishonour the giant's memory.

At an old mound called MwaNunuauNunuauau we learnt more about funeral rites. Corpses were first washed on stones and then the body laid over a deep hole nearby. As the flesh rotted it was picked off by special attendants who were not allowed to show any revulsion. If they did so, they paid shell money as compensation or were killed. When the flesh had rotted the long leg and arm bones were hidden in caves, while the jawbone was hung in the descendant's hut to provide protection.

John led us back past the villagers' gardens to the nearest bush settlement Dahui, which had been established in 1910. There were coconuts, sago palms, betelnuts and bananas in the nearby bush.

The settlement was established after a dysentery outbreak in nine outlying hamlets which killed many and drove one hundred people into Dahui. Another thirty people died in Dahui before it was abandoned in 1915.

It was thought dysentery was introduced by around thirty deserters from whaling ships who took up residence in Arosi for twenty years from the 1850s.[105]

Makira was also visited by blackbirding ships whose captains enticed men on board and sailed off with them to the sugar cane plantations of Queensland. In Makira it is possible that up to one-third of the population died of dysentery.[106]

The move to the coast accelerated after 1918 when Frederick Campbell was appointed as the first district officer in Kirakira. He divided Makira into eight regions, appointed district chiefs and encouraged people to move to the coast where they could be more readily taxed and evangelised.

George's maternal family history was linked to that of Frederick Campbell, and Father Abel told me how this South Malaitan family arrived in Makira.

In 1908 Sahu had been in the hills of South Malaita with his sister when she saw a great boat with sails. While she and the rest of the family fled to the hills, Sahu returned to the deserted village. Before leaving, his sister blessed him and prayed for his protection. Someone in their family had beheaded a sorcerer. They suspected this man of casting a spell over one of their kinsmen who had died after a long illness.

Sahu watched the soldiers arrive together with one of his brothers who spoke a little English. Sahu was surprised when they grabbed him and even more surprised when they came from his hut with the head of the murdered man in his bag. He looked for his brother, but he had fled.

Sahu's hands were tied behind him, he was marched to the boat and thrown in. At first he was very angry, but as he lay in the tiny dark locked room he became afraid. There was a great gale, the room rocked wildly, and he was sick. He didn't eat their bread or drink their water.

Instead he lay on the floor wishing he was dead, believing they would kill him anyway.

Two things comforted him, his sister's blessing and the strange impulse which led him back to the village. Finally in the early morning he was taken on deck. It was only then, watching the sun rising surrounded by wispy clouds, he was glad to be alive.

At the settlement he saw white men's houses made of big cut logs. He was locked in a dark room so small he could barely stretch out. He shivered despite the heat. Every day they bought him a small bowl of thin soup and emptied his pan. One day they took him upstairs and he sat in front of a fat white man. He understood nothing and was taken back to his room.

One night he had a dream. He was almost dead, but someone carried him back to a hut and nursed him. He knew then he would live. From that day he began to receive large chunks of coconut in his soup. One day something crashed through his window. It was a bible in his own language. Time passed more easily as he struggled to read it and listened to those outside talking in English and pidgin. He asked and found someone to bring him a pen and paper and slowly taught himself how to write.

One day he woke to hear a bird singing and pulled himself up by the bars to watch it. Every day he watched as the bird made a nest, laid its eggs and fed its chicks.

When he was released, he almost fainted in the great gust of air and space. The bushes beside his room which had been tiny when he entered were now great blossom covered trees. He was elated. He had paid the price for the sin that had been committed, but no-one would ever trample on him again.

Sahu spent ten years in prison and never returned to South Malaita.

Instead, he became friends with Frederick Campbell, who was posted to Kirakira as district commissioner in Kirakira in 1918 and later became a planter. Sahu was encouraged by Frederick to accompany him from Tulagi, where he had been imprisoned, to Kirakira.

Frederick then asked Sahu to go to Arosi and set up a store. In Arosi, Sahu married a local girl whose mother was from South Malaita and they had children, one of whom was Rebi.[107]

Another person who had a great influence on the Arosi area was a European priest, Charles Fox. He arrived in the Solomons in 1908, the same year that Sahu was imprisoned. He was an Anglican missionary who remained in the Solomons for sixty-five years until 1973.

He was in Makira from 1911 to 1924 where he opened the first boarding school in the Solomons in Pamua. The school had guards as bushmen threatened Fox's life, and during a raid beheaded one woman.[108]

He had retired to Auckland when I met George but was often spoken of in Tawatana. Michael Scott wrote about Dr Fox and included his meeting with two former teachers in Tawatana, Mr Ben and Madam Sarah. They described how they had met Doctor Fox in the sixties and were surprised at his old version of Arosi, which they barely understood.

Scott said locals believed Dr Fox received his spiritual power after he undertook a name changing ceremony with Martin Taki. This included a complete swap of their lifestyles and possessions. While Martin lived in Dr Fox's house and took over not only his possessions, but his bank account of forty pounds, Dr Fox took over Martin's hut and yam garden. From then on, Dr Fox said he lived as a native and was regarded as such.[ibid]

While Sahu had died long before I got to the Solomons, George remembered him as a very powerful custom medicine man and a shark caller. George was very sick when he was a child and was sent to the hospital in Kirakira.

They sent him back to the village and as he was still sick, he was sent to see his grandfather. His grandfather chided the doctors, saying it was just a 'baby sick' and promptly cured him.

Kaha or May, George's paternal grandmother, was still alive when the children and I visited. She was going blind from cataracts but finally had surgery. There is a photo of her looking resolutely at the camera with large thick rimmed glasses, lenses which replaced her own lenses.

She was often cold, especially at night, and lived with her son Barnabas and his wife Eunice. They put a fireplace in her bedroom with a chimney. When I left the village, she alone was allowed to use my toilet.

I was taken to the custom court following the incident when the house girl and I sat on a log that was to become a rafter. We had climbed a steep muddy path and when we found the log at the top, sat on it. That meant it could no longer be used, as custom decreed a man could not stand underneath anything a woman had touched. I pleaded ignorance and was let off with a warning.

I updated mum about Haruta and his magnificent garden. His wife kept packing her bags, running away and then returning. He was very distressed because he had some yams which spoiled while waiting for planting.

I continued saying George had a tough time while we were away, winning at gambling and paying some debts. I learnt many years later that my parents had sent him the money. He was now able to pay the Provincial Press and the paper was to be printed the following week.

> My salary will come from office cleaning which is going OK while his will come from the paper. The News Drum has stopped production while a private group organises itself.
>
> A very capable minister in Mamaloni's Government has resigned saying he can't work with the rest of the cabinet. The political situation is pretty shaky. George will cover it next week. I am feeling cheerful again and looking forward to struggling with George.[109]

A week later on 21 May 1982, I had looked at George's books and discovered his many debts:

> He has received an impressive array of threatening letters. I am sending a circular to the creditors asking them to be patient and advising I will pay as soon as possible. I will allocate $300 a month for debts and estimate it will take a year to pay them. I have sorted out the tax and NPF (a compulsory superannuation fund). I am taking $200 a month salary from office cleaning which is making a profit.
>
> I think the business will be all right. We need to collect $650 advertising a week. We have $800 ads for next week.
>
> The children are doing well. I have been so involved with the business I haven't seen much of them. I don't go home at lunchtime now and spend one or two evenings a week supervising the cleaning. Brian was three the other day. Unfortunately, he doesn't go to kindergarten anymore as I have no way of getting him down there. The baby is a very bright little boy. I am still breastfeeding him.
>
> Politics is shaky. A very able minister has resigned and called for the PM's resignation.
>
> It is a strain typing this but I feel I have to improve my typing.[110].

I will never forget a couple of weeks later I was cleaning late at night. Seeing some flowers and a calendar on an office desk I realised it was 2 June, my birthday. I burst into tears.

Two days later I wrote:

I have just survived the hardest two to three weeks of my life. I hope the worst is now over. I had to get on the street and beg for advertisements and win back the advertisers' confidence. I also had to win over the Development Bank and the printer.

The Development Bank will let us have the printing press back as soon as we erect a wall in the office to put it behind. The Government Printer will come and sort out the machine, maintain the machines and give us small jobs. They will tell us exactly what sort of dark room equipment we need.

We will typeset the paper ourselves on our own typewriter and save $120 a week and will be using an unofficial photographer (we will give him some bulbs) who said he would improve the quality and number of photos. The rival paper doesn't seem to have come out this week.

We will be paying the bank $100 to $200 a month so hopefully that is OK. There may be prospects to provide office services typing etc.

The company which was taking George to court for a $400 debt didn't turn up so the case was dismissed.

It is hard, but I hope things will improve soon.[111]

Two weeks in which I was humbled by the Solomon

Islanders' belief that now I was involved the business would be okay.

> As soon as they knew I had joined George, people in the offices and on the streets said, 'It will be all right in a few months'. While others have confidence in me, I have little in myself. People who owed George money have paid it and people are giving us food and all sorts of things. Our workers weren't paid last month but will be at the end of this week.
> I am surviving on $200 a month from office cleaning services. I have got a few companies interested and there is the possibility we will get a floor polisher. I am not so desperate now. I am so busy with the newspaper by day and office cleaning by night I see little of the children and can't get Brian to kindergarten.[112]

A month later, I had been become a reporter and was happy with the quality of the stories we were writing. We worked all weekend and I wrote on 12 July:

> On Saturday morning I do the accounts and in the afternoon I write up the stories I've collected. On Monday they are typeset. We are getting quite a few ads. If George can manage to get $300 a month salary we will be all right. He will put it into my bank account and I will manage it.
> We are living as simply as possible eating rice and

second grade taiyo (cheap local canned fish) every night. The paper is slowly struggling to its feet. I'm doing a lot of writing and people say it is improving. We are in the process of organising the cheapest good builder. The former builder died. His son will probably take over. (This was for an office building my parents had sent money for. Full point inside bracket and not after). I have never regretted my decision to leave the hospital and feel a lot freer and happier in many ways.[113]

Two weeks later an MP praised the *Toktok* and *Observer* for 'their fair reporting'.[114]

A couple of days later I spoke of our competition, the *Solomon Star*:

> The other paper is selling very well, not so much because of their content but their World Cup soccer photos. They have been constantly criticising the government.
>
> The Prime Minister slammed them in his independence anniversary speech while one minister is suing them for $2,500 for defamation.
>
> The wife of the editor is depressed about it. I said we would do what we could to help without prejudicing our own paper.[115]

When the head of school and I left, all the work that had gone into revising the nursing curriculum was lost and I reported on 21 July 1982:

The Minister of Health has approved the decision that general nurse training be suspended while the curriculum is revised.

The Permanent Secretary for Health and Medical Services Albert Manira said the present curriculum was inadequate because trainees were missing vital rural experience. He said the present standard of nursing in the rural areas is unsatisfactory showing the curriculum is inadequate. However the revised general curriculum was introduced in 1980 and the first intake of students will not graduate until the end of this year.

Mr Manira was therefore asked how this curriculum could be evaluated.

He replied it is unsatisfactory and will be assessed and changed by local nursing personnel next year. Instead of training first-year nursing students the ministry will concentrate on raising the standard of nurses already registered, he said. The second- and thirdyear nursing students will continue their training.[116]

The National Development Bank contacted George again, noting it had seen an improvement in the quality of the paper. The advertising revenue had increased to around $800 a week, while printing costs were $380. Our circulation had increased from 1000 to 1,500 and the extra copies were selling fast.[117]

It was very hard work, as I told my mother who was then in New Zealand:

> I am working up to fourteen hour days. I spent yesterday, Saturday on accounting, and I seem to be passing. (I had begun an online accountancy course from Massey University which I subsequently dropped.)
>
> We then rushed up the hill and planted some cassava so we have a few vegetables in four months. Then I wrote a feature for next week. Then I tried to repair my knickers which are in their last stages.
>
> The baby at nine-and-a-half nine and a half months is climbing everything and Brian is roaming around with the neighbouring children. They suffer from not seeing us a lot. One night a week I come home very late after cleaning while George lays out the paper. That can take all night, even two nights.[118]

I was nicknamed the barefoot reporter, not because I had no shoes, but because I had no transport and I walked. I was accessible and people gave me tips. Already the effects of the high birth rate and the population inflow from the rural areas were beginning to test the infrastructure.

> Many Honiara children who are eligible to go to primary school could be turned away next year. This is because there is an acute shortage of classroom space and not enough money to build new ones.
>
> A spokesperson for the Education Division of the Honiara Municipal Authority said World Vision would provide $23,000 to build two classrooms each for five

Honiara schools but it was unclear when the money would be available.

The spokesperson said if the situation becomes critical it may be necessary to hold morning and evening school, with the same teachers teaching both.[119]

I also covered health related stories the other media didn't:

The Red Cross Handicapped Centre staff have pleaded for parents of the children who attend to come and watch their children's progress. Manager Catherine Amasia said children only spend a few hours there and their parents need to continue their program at home.

There are seven deaf children attending and Miss Amasia said if the parents taught them at home, holding up objects and speaking clearly, they would be able to attend public schools as they do in Fiji.[120]

My parents were curious as to why our financial situation was so tight. I explained it was because we were paying off the accumulated debts of the past six years. The cleaning business was on a much more secure footing, and I had contracts of $700 a month. The business was more technical than I expected as I explained below in relation to the vinyl tiles in the HK bank in a letter written in mid-August:

The builders put the wrong type of wax on, and the floors

looked terrible. Three boys and I spent ten hours each over Friday and the weekend, on our knees, getting the wax off with cloudy ammonia. We left it for ten minutes, washed it off with water and then applied three coats of vinyl polish with intervals of twenty minutes in between. The floors certainly now look a lot better.

They are giving me a month's trial and if that goes well will give me a contract for a year at $200 a month.

We are just about supporting ourselves now. I would say we are about $40 a month short. I am handling the household budget and am very strict. At least our eating has improved.

The Australian High Commissioner took George, Ida and the children out for a feast at a village yesterday. I was in the bank cleaning! Brian really enjoyed it.

He was very cheerful after 'the ride in the car'. I think I will send him to kindergarten next month despite the $40 a month shortfall.

Because we are working so hard, we are both rather tired and crochety. Still, I respect George's judgement. I would feel nervous about putting in a story he hadn't seen.[121]

Life in Vura could be unpredictable.

One of our neighbours came over and threatened to kill

me (I'm not sure why). He also threatened my house cleaner over a very trivial incident, and since she has left I have been doing the cleaning myself.

There are now six large men from South Malaita 'visiting' the man who threatened us this morning. This society has its own ways of protecting people. Hopefully it will be straightened out so I can find someone else to help with the house.[122]

George was impressed by some of the *Star*'s scoops and wrote an editorial on 9 September 1982 congratulating them:

Solomons Toktok congratulates the *Solomons Star* on running the story about the $200 million loan. In presenting that story the paper is carrying out one of the functions of the media, to be a watchdog.

The Solomons *Star* has recently run a series of stories of national importance including the increase in MPs' terminal grants, the employment of Mr da Silva and the problem of the government having no nuclear policy when there was a nuclear armed ship at Point Cruz.[123]

In early October, George was overseas for a few weeks and I was running the *Toktok* and the cleaning on my own, including laying the paper out and taking pictures. I was looking forward to his return on the thirteenth of the month.

I was also indignant that I had to pay twenty per cent duty for my cleaning materials while they charged five per cent for opium and cocaine:

> On Saturday I had to clean the HK Bank so I took Brian with me. He thoroughly enjoyed himself mopping and helping and was disappointed we weren't going again on Sunday.[124]

On 18 October 1982 the Queen and Duke of Edinburgh arrived.

> Well, the Queen has come and gone. George and I spent all day trailing after her with the overseas reporters and photographers. It was quite exhausting.
> I also followed the Duke of Edinburgh when he toured the hospital. He asked about the birth rate, which at 3.4 per cent is one of the highest in the world. He made one of his pithy remarks, like 'they must be mad'. He also complained about not being able to buy a decent pair of shoes in Honiara. I wondered why he hadn't bought them in London before he came. I asked his aide for a more pertinent comment about unsustainable logging, but he turned me down.[125]

Sir Peter Kenilorea was the only politician at that time who was concerned about the birth rate.

He told a press conference in January 1983 that

resources and services in the country could not cope with the high rate of population growth. The long-term difficulties which included a shortage of schools, clinics and hospitals, should be brought to people's attention.

Sir Peter said the nation had a Planned Parenthood Association but its role was different. It believed a couple could have ten children as long as they were well cared for, and their mother remained healthy.[126]

Prime Minister Solomon Mamaloni told me during an interview in April he wasn't concerned and neither it appeared was the Solomon Islands Broadcasting Authority. In December 1982 it broadcast erroneous information claiming that Depo-provera, an injectable contraceptive, caused cancer. I quickly contacted the Solomon Islands Planned Parenthood Association (SIPPA) for a statement:

> There is no evidence to show the Depo-provera injection used in family planning has ever caused one case of cancer of the uterus or the womb, a recent International Planned Parenthood Federation Report states. Depo-provera is the injection used every three months to prevent women getting pregnant. When they stop the injection 92 to 97 women out of a hundred get pregnant within two years.

In December 1982, the Solomon Islands Broadcasting Corporation (SIBC) said the Solomon Islands Planned Parent Association (SIPPA) had banned Depo-provera because it caused cancer. The SIBC said they had contacted a nurse at SIPPA and advised her Depo-provera had been banned in other countries because of the cancer risk and asked if it was banned in the Solomons. The SIPPA nurse advised them to contact the SIPPA doctor, Dr Maemaruki. They did not contact him.

The SIPPA spokesperson said Depo-provera had not been banned and they were aware it did not cause cancer. Health authorities are concerned because increasing numbers of women are refusing Depo-provera.[127]

I don't know that the SIBC ever retracted its statement. Years later in rural Makira, the idea was still entrenched.

In May 1983, I carried out a street poll about family planning. Not surprisingly, most women were in favour of it, however the men either hadn't heard of it or didn't support it.

> A street poll about family planning showed that while it was overwhelmingly supported by twenty of the twenty-one women interviewed, almost half of the twenty-eight men interviewed either didn't know what it was, or didn't support it.
>
> One young man interviewed wanted to start an army, while another said there was a lot of land in the Solomons and not enough people. Another male interviewed said family planning had too many side effects and the government should get more foreign companies to invest to provide work for the extra babies born. Four men from

rural areas had never heard of family planning, because they didn't have radios.

The women interviewed were adamant that couples should have the number of children they could care for and support financially. They said the best sized family was from two to five children. One woman said she had eight children and would have preferred four, as they were short of money.[128]

This population growth has led to an explosion of young people. In 2018, seven out of ten Solomon Islanders were under thirty, and there was a youth unemployment rate of more than thirty-five per cent[129]. Although youths are finding it difficult to get work, they are attending primary school in greater numbers. While in 1982 less than half of the children between seven and nineteen went to primary school, [130] this increased to 94 per cent in 2010.[131]

Another statistic which has improved is the number of people getting malaria. In 1982, there were 70,000 officially recorded malaria cases with three hundred people out of every thousand getting malaria that year.[132] By 2017 that had dropped to ninety out of one thousand people.[133]

*

While I worked as a journalist with George as editor, the paper and our marriage thrived. There was a fire in Chinatown in February 1983. I wrote the lead article after interviewing John Gatu, assistant superintendent of the Solomon Islands fire brigade and George followed up with an article about the financial cost of the fire and lessons learnt:

> The fire was the biggest the country had experienced and was fought by the public. They crowded around the burning DLK buildings until bullets started going off. A gang of twenty boys ripped the axes off the fire engine, climbed on to the roof and began chopping.
>
> This made the fire worse, and they were lucky it didn't explode, Mr Gatu said. Another group rushed into a smoke-filled building to loot. Somehow, they avoided being overcome by smoke inhalation from the burning plastics and were also lucky the burning roof didn't fall on them.
>
> The fire was well advanced by the time the fire service arrived. The police were notified first, but as their alarm to the fire station was not working a policeman had to run there. The five fire trucks then couldn't access the fire because of the crowds. After emptying their tanks, they refilled them from the nearby Mataniko river, and this took fifteen minutes. Nature finally intervened with a heavy shower near midnight, and the fire was extinguished two hours later.[134]

George in his commentary said Chinatown was unsafe with its old wooden buildings crowded together. He also questioned the storage of ammunitions and gas in an unsafe manner and said it was lucky a petrol depot twenty yards away had not caught fire.[135]

I was also covering the courts:

> A fifteen-year-old youth was unlawfully arrested and detained by the police.
>
> Chief Justice Francis Daly released him last week because the police could not produce sufficient evidence he killed a man at Tasifarongo Plantation last year.
>
> He was brought to Honiara on 31 October after an identification parade of labourers during which the killer was not identified.
>
> Justice Daly told the court the youth was put in a solitary cell for six days with no explanation. He was fed four biscuits and one small can of fish daily. On 6 November he was interviewed by Sergeant Talu and one other police officer and confessed to the crime. He was finally taken to court nine days after he was put in prison.
>
> The Chief Justice said he has neither the experience, education nor intelligence to understand police procedures. He can sign his name but cannot read or write. He ruled he could not accept the material in the confession as evidence against the youth.[136]

Prime Minister Solomon Mamaloni grew weary of my 'investigative journalism' and I was told to get my stories vetted by the Government Information Service. My strategy was to approach them with five to six leads as sometimes leads petered out. By the sixth, they would glaze over and I would brightly ask when they wanted to see me again. They would mumble about their own work, and I would leave without another appointment.

By March, we had increased our copies to two thousand weekly and George was about to travel to a conference in Cyprus, staying with my parents in Hong Kong on the way back. The political situation was shaky and corruption was becoming more evident:

> The Prime Minister is trying to reshuffle his cabinet, but the ministers refuse to move. He is also offside with the finance minister, and it is beginning to feel as if he has lost control. Some of the ministers are definitely 'off'. We are running three stories about corruption next week.
>
> Here the power seems to lie with the Minister of Finance, and to some extent the Leader of the Opposition, the law (under a lot of pressure) and us, the press.
>
> I am sticking closely to the lawyers from the Public Solicitors Office. They are having a rough time as the politicians are trying to remove them. I don't know when the pressure is going to start falling on us. They're kicking an independent newspaper out of Vanuatu – however, apparently the editor was fed information by politicians about a corruption issue which was already a year old.
>
> I'm seeing quite a lot of the diplomats here. They have a far better grasp of what's going on than I have. One of

them wants to help with establishing a refuge for domestic violence. There's a lot of it here and these women have nowhere to go. Many of them are working women and have to stay in town.[137]

In mid-May I finally managed to get an interview with the prime minister, quite an achievement considering his attitude to the media.

Under Mamaloni's leadership logging grew, with the number of logging licences quadrupling between 1981 and 1983.[138] One of the reasons was because customary landowners could set up logging companies under the North New Georgia Timber Corporation Act (1982).

Previously the provincial government had been involved with the approval, but this was overturned when landowners in New Georgia destroyed a Levers Pacific Timbers logging camp and the above Act was passed.

Mamaloni admitted landowners and logging companies sometimes dropped in on him and members of the Investment Advisory Committee (the approval body), attempting to influence the outcome.[139]

Because of the rapid increase in logging licences granted in 1982 the Solomon Islands Ministry of Lands, Energy and National Resources reported the total licence quota issued was 495,000 cubic metres, more than the sustainable annual limit of 360,000 cubic metres.[140]

It was clear not enough provision was made for replanting. The Governor of the Central Bank, Tony

Hughes, pointed out in the bank's annual report in 1982 that 9000 hectares of forest was being logged annually. To replace this, plantation forests of 3000 hectares annually were needed. In 1981 and 1982, the government replanted 500 hectares each year at an annual cost of $1.35 million. During 1982, government revenues from timber export duty and royalties on public land was $2.7 million. Even if this revenue was used for replanting it would only cover 1000 hectares annually, leaving a shortfall of 2000 hectares.[141]

One solution was to get the companies concerned to reforest. The logging companies were not interested, while a multinational company, Unilever, said there was not enough government security provided for long-term investment.

They expressed interest in reforesting 16,000 hectares of land, but a spokesperson said:

> Who would want to invest in the timber industry in the Solomon Islands? It is easier to run a logging operation. You load your equipment on to a couple of barges and walk in. Any trouble and you load it back on to the barges.[142]

In Fiji, a statutory commission, the Fiji Pine Commission was formed. This was the approach two advisers from the Food and Agricultural Organisation (FAO) recommended for the Solomons following a field survey.[143] The consultants said a Solomon Islands State Forestry Commission could act as an intermediary between timber companies and landowners ensuring the companies got security and the landowners a fair deal.

Other responsibilities could include advising the government on forest policy and licensing and supervising existing and future logging and processing industries. This body could assist with the development of small sawmills and support landowners with replanting. It would identify and safeguard forest and wildlife needing protection. The study said the commission would be profitable, could borrow money, enter joint ventures and attract aid.[144]

The website of the Fiji Pine Commission, which was accessed in March 2022, shows what an opportunity the Solomons missed. Sustainable and certified forestry ensures the country retains one hundred per cent of their export income and generates foreign exchange from sawn timbers and woodchips.[145]

Mamaloni also devolved further powers to the provinces as Tony Hughes pointed out in the Central Bank's 1982 annual report. In 1982, the central government grants to provincial assemblies were $5.9 million or 85 per cent of their income. Five-hundred public officers were seconded to the provincial governments at a cost of $3.1 million. One quarter of the national government income went to the provinces.

During 1982, the government partly cancelled debts owed by the provincial governments. Remaining debts were transferred to the Provincial Assemblies Loans fund on fixed-repayment terms. The amount of debt provinces owed central government fell during 1982 and reflected better financial control in most provinces.[146]

However, this was not what the Auditor General's team found when they visited five provincial secondary schools in 1982:

> An auditor's report on the construction and extension of provincial secondary schools during the last three years, recommends that no further government finance is provided until financial accountability and construction is improved.
>
> The audit team visited five provincial secondary schools, Choiseul, Avuavu, Rokera, Siota and Pawa. They said in every case, provincial assemblies did not have the manpower, machinery or expertise to carry out the program efficiently, in the time frame and within budget.
>
> The team visited Pawa in 1982 which had extensive damage after Cyclone Kerry. Twelve-thousand-and-two-hundred dollars was made available for rebuilding. No accounts were kept by the province. Although two boys' dormitories were built, these had no floor, no ceilings, no window shutters and were unfurnished. One girls' dormitory was also built and had no louvres.
>
> In February 1980 a further $15,000 was provided to build a library, low-cost houses, and buy a freezer, fridge and sewing machines.

When the audit team visited there was no evidence of these buildings or items and no evidence of how the money had been spent.[147]

When I interviewed Mamaloni I asked how the central government disciplined provinces. He replied if they broke the law, the Provincial Government Act would be invoked and if it was administrative the Public Service Office would be involved.

In an attempt to curb inflation, a Price Control Act was implemented in 1983. This resulted in a shortage of sugar, tinned fish and meat. This was because business owners had to sell them at a loss.

A wholesaler explained that Imperial Corned beef was landed at $1.09 a tin and the maximum sale price allowed under the Price Control Act was $1.04 a tin. The wholesaler said wholesalers needed a 10-12 per cent profit on their goods. A small shopkeeper stated he needed a profit margin of 20 to 25 per cent. Most of this would be absorbed by operating costs and from this there would be a two- to three per cent profit.

The Secretary to the Price Control Committee, Diane Kerwin, said the shortage had occurred because the prices set were three months out of date. Costs had risen because Australian beef prices were higher following the end of a seven-year drought, freight costs were higher and the exchange rates had changed. A report was prepared by the Price Control Committee on May 4 and they were waiting for the Minister of Finance Mr Bartholomew Ulufa'alu to return from overseas to present it to him.

There was a complaint to the *Toktok* that the price of 777 fish was not controlled and yet it was the most popular canned fish. Mrs Kerwin said this was her mistake. When she did her initial survey there was little 777 fish in the shops because it was so popular.[148]

George had been away for six weeks and I had the financial side under control, but I was exhausted. I realised I had established my reputation as a journalist when I met Robert Reid, from *Pacific Business*, one of the Pacific's best monthlies, and was asked to write one to three features a month. The problem was time.

George was still away and in mid-May mum wrote to her sister Diana in Oman describing me as gloomy. She said George was staying with them and had gone to Canton for a couple of days. She added I had applied for a three-month scholarship with New Zealand newspapers at the end of the year.[149]

A week later George arrived back, and Jane (the advertising manager) and I decided we would handle the money while George remained editor. My application for the traineeship with New Zealand newspapers was successful and I was looking forward to a break.

Chapter 7

NZ TRAINING, RETURN TO SOLOMONS AND FLIGHT

The Commonwealth Press scholarship I received was to work with three newspapers, the *Wellington Evening Post*, the *Christchurch Star* and the *Christchurch Press* from July to October 1983. It was this three-month absence from the Solomons that ripped our marriage apart. Not only did the children mourn my absence, but I also recognise now, George did too. Things fell apart at the office and home because I was the centre of both. On reflection perhaps I shouldn't have gone, but there was no hesitation at the time from either myself or George. Eunice told me later that I should have sent the children to Taroniara.

Before I left, the YWCA asked me to attend a national conference on rape and violence organised by the New Zealand YWCA. They were unable to afford to send a representative. However, when I attended, the organisers forbade me to attend the Maori and Pacific Islanders sessions because I was white. It was a confronting conference as I described in an article for the *Christchurch*

Press called the 'Militant Faction'. However, there were some good outcomes including the recommendation the police be asked to recruit more women.

I also interviewed a very fine Maori leader, Mira Szaszy, one of the first Maori women university graduates. She was founder of the Maori Women's League, had advocated for Maori play centres and Maori housing and had started a specialist home for Maori victims of incest.

I wrote to dad in August from Christchurch. Mum had flown to New Plymouth where her mother was dying:

> I am enjoying the *Star*. I attended a very dull meeting of the North Canterbury Parks and Reserves Board and managed to get a story about how the rangers sprayed some endangered plants while they were spraying for gorse. The chief reporter from the *Star* has a girlfriend from the *Press* who was there too, but she had gone to sleep.[150]

I was tired and would have liked a break, but I received an urgent telegram from Jane asking that I return immediately.

Returning to the Solomons was awful. The children looked like waifs. I was told every time a plane flew over, they would look at it and wonder if mummy was on it. Nason had looked after them and said George had not been at home much.

In the office, Jane and the rest of the staff refused to work with George. It appeared to be about money. George told me it wasn't nice to walk around as the managing director and not have a penny in his pocket. The cleaners too were happy to see me and were short of supplies.

I got straight back into the daily routine, beginning with health-related stories:

> The Minister of Health, George Suri is considering asking antenatal patients, admitted to the maternity ward by doctors, to pay. Some of these patients have recently been admitted to the private ward as there is no room in the public maternity ward. These are women with complications which endanger their lives and that of their unborn baby. Many of them do not have the money to pay.
>
> Hospital staff are very concerned about the minister's proposed action and were planning to hold a demonstration on October 21, but it did not go ahead due to government intervention.[151]

The children and I went by boat to Gela a week after I arrived in early November to meet George. Before I left Honiara Jane told me about the financial problems including the publication of overseas advertisements which had not been paid for. I wrote:

> After four days in Gela, I am finally relaxing. It is very beautiful here and Barnabas and Eunice have a very comfortable house. I'm afraid it does look like our marriage is coming to an end. We have not been able to communicate for a long time and I don't think that

will change. However, I would like to leave things in a reasonable state.

Rebi is now here which I find a great comfort. She is a fine old woman. I think she realises what the situation is although we haven't talked about it. She's sensible enough to realise it's no-one's fault.

I then discuss a number of scenarios and say of the children:

John at two is quite a handful and loves his father. Brian at four is very sensible. He's rather bossy I'm afraid and insecure about me now. He wants to know where I am all the time. I'm in a perfectly reasonable frame of mind and feel I can cope with everything with your support.[152]

It was clear to me I would have to go. I didn't respect George anymore and I was very angry about the state I found the children in.

Rebi was so wise. It was very brave of her to come to Honiara because she had never left Makira before. I did tell her I was leaving, which was a risk, because expatriate women and their children had been stopped at the border before and we were a high-profile family.

Rebi said she loved both of us and was very sad I was going. I was very sorry George would have difficulty seeing his children but professionally and personally I could not see a future for us in the Solomons.

Work was a solace. There was a difference in the

effectiveness of the financial management in some provinces, as I reported on 17 November 1983:

> The Guadalcanal province was down to its last couple of hundred dollars early this month and released this information to the Solomon Islands Broadcasting Service on November 9. After the media release the national government paid the October instalment together with reimbursement money which totalled $37,000. Reuben Teilo treasurer of the Guadalcanal Province said the allowance was paid late and the province spent money on capital projects which he felt the National Government should have provided money for.[153]

The budget shortage and management shortcomings also affected the vehicle supply and touring program of agricultural extension workers in Guadalcanal:

> The agricultural extension officers in Guadalcanal have no vehicle. Their recently purchased Land Rover is undergoing repairs at a private station. The principal field officer, Kaura Tioti, said the driver damaged the vehicle crossing a river. Mr Tioti said there needed to be further regulations and training around load limits and river crossings. The vehicle is used for transporting fertiliser and fencing wire to substations and farmers.
> The division consisting of 19 senior staff seconded from the government and 24 provincial employees also

has six canoes and engines, however only three of the engines are working.

Mr Tioti said the Public Works Division does not maintain provincial canoe engines and vehicles and the provincial mechanic does not have the expertise and equipment to do it.

Field staff continue to tour without a vehicle and despite no touring allowances being paid since August. They use other provincial vehicles or private transport. As only half the canoes are in use, they often walk a couple of days to the farmers and cannot take the fertiliser and fencing wire farmers have ordered.[154]

While Guadalcanal was struggling, Malaita was not having financial difficulties. The Minister of Finance, Bart Ulufa'alu, picked up the theme in a radio interview, and admitted there was a need to upgrade financial management in the provinces.

In the same issue I wrote an editorial about the availability of public service accountants in the Solomons:

> There are only two accountants with metropolitan accounting qualifications in the public service. Next year, there will be only one. This does not include the Auditor General and Accounts Trainer who work directly with Government Finances.
>
> The need to train Solomon Islands accountants at full speed is apparent and the formation of the Solomon

Islands Institute of Accountants is an important step in this direction. The first five-year-long Solomon Islands course in accounting will begin at the new College of Advanced Education in 1985. Meanwhile, it is essential the government recruit more expatriate accountants.[155]

Below is the story titled *Mi Mere*, or *I Am Woman*, which I alluded to in the previous chapter when Sue and I went to Tulagi together. I am still moved when I read it:

> *Mi Mere* or *I Am Woman*, breathes with the thoughts and feelings of Solomon Islands women. Clearly, simply and movingly they portray themselves.
>
> This book is a very 'democratic' one. It is published by the USP Solomon Islands Centre and edited by Afu Billy, Hazel Lulei and Jully Sipolo.
>
> It was compiled after two women's writers' workshops in 1980 and 1981. It is divided into six parts and I have chosen to review *Olketa Man*, a subject which has puzzled women for thousands of years.
>
> A photo under the title by Sue Fleming shows a doorway. Through this can be seen a cross-legged male holding his male child upright. I like Sue Fleming's photos. While the Information Service photos sometimes seem disembodied, the head has lost its body, the figure has lost its surroundings, her photos are never like this. There is a tenderness about them and a regard for the people and their life. We see coconut brooms, leaf huts, kumara

peelings, the life we all know, so familiar, and now seen in a new light.

An anonymous story titled *Big Brother*, tells of a man who has gained prestige in the European world, but sadly appears to have lost his humanity and respect for his people. It is anonymous because this is a small country and as the preface explains, there are still 'real constraints on the freedom of expression of women in Solomon Islands society.'

Ellen Fera has written a poem, *I Can't Wait Any Longer*, about the slow growth of love between a man and a woman. A simple poem which portrays accurately feelings many women must have experienced. Together with a short story titled *As I Remember My Father*, they are the only contributions in this section which uncomplainingly accept men. Victoria Analau has a fine father, a man prepared to stand by his principles and religion under adverse circumstances.

The other stories puzzle over men. Men obtain education and a chasm opens between them and their family. They are confused. They beat their women.

They have other priorities such as sports, as shown in a moving poem by Jully Sipolo about her brother.[156]

In mid-November I approached the Public Solicitor's office and asked about divorce. I was surprised to learn I had never been married and wrote to my parents:

I got married in the village under the Native Marriage Ordinance Act and needless to say I am not a native. I am tired and demoralised and so is George. We have agreed we will eventually separate but not until everything is sorted out. Rebi is still here.[157]

The following week, I outline a plan:

> Thanks for your letters. It's Sunday and I'm tired. Parliament is sitting and there are all sorts of grievous things going on. I'm tired of carrying a community on my shoulders and it feels inappropriate. I am drifting towards returning to NZ. I was very happy there and feel we would be more settled.
>
> I know I could set up the printing and probably make a success of it. The business community are behind us as are some of the Australians and even some of the politicians. However, I am not happy and know how unstable it is. Because of my unhappy situation with George, the Prime Minister could decide not to grant me a work permit, and it could all come tumbling down. Also, there is the problem of the children's education.
>
> I would like to go back to Wellington. I could work as a nurse while I sort out something in journalism.
>
> Also, Eve, Clare and Steven are there (my maternal aunt and cousins). I might need a month or two in HK before I go back though. I will be exhausted.[158]

This was the plan we followed.

I may have needed a work permit to work in the country, but the Chief Justice ruled in the case below that expatriate women married to Solomon Islanders did not need a residency permit.

This case occurred when government officials took a heavily pregnant woman to the airport to deport her. The airline refused to accept her and the next day she married her Solomon Islands partner:

> A deportation order made by the Minister of Police and Justice Allen Qurusu, on 26 October was quashed by the High Court on 17 November. The deportation order was made against Mrs M, from Tarawa.
>
> Government officials took Mrs M to Henderson Airport on 26 October to put her on an Air Nauru flight but the airline officials refused to take her as she is due to give birth by the end of this month.
>
> That afternoon she married a Solomon Islander and as she is now married, she is no longer a prohibited immigrant. Chief Justice Daly also found that she does not need a permit to reside in the Solomon Islands.
>
> James Apaniai, who appeared for the Attorney General, argued that expatriate wives of Solomon Islanders under the age of eighteen did not need a permit but women above eighteen do.
>
> Chief Justice Daly said this would mean that Solomon Islanders who wished to marry expatriate women would

have to rely on approval from the Minister of Immigration. This would be discrimination against Solomon Islands citizens.

Public Solicitor Andrew Radclyffe submitted that at the time the deportation order was made on 26 October the minister was in possession of chief magistrate Tony Parker's report.

That report documented that the woman intended to marry a Solomon Islands citizen on 28 October and she was due to give birth in a matter of weeks. She had another child by her first marriage to a Solomon Islander who she would never see again if she was deported.

Mr Radclyffe said if she had been deported on 26 October, a future Solomon Islands citizen, the unborn child, would be deprived of its right to a future in the Solomon Islands.[159]

I was tired of men, including politicians, talking about women's liberation in a derogatory way and decided to address the issue in an editorial on 24 November:

> Women's Liberation has become a dirty word in the Solomons. At a USP (University of the South Pacific) graduation midyear, the Prime Minister warned female graduates they had not been educated so they could practise women's lib.
>
> Staff writer Margaret Atkin is constantly being accused of being a women's libber so let's look at the

meaning of the word liberation. Liberation, according to the *Oxford Dictionary*, means 'to set at liberty, to free from oppressive social conditions.'

So what is so frightful about allowing women to take their place alongside men and participate in the development of this country? As women are half the population, they are a resource this country cannot afford to neglect. Perhaps Solomon Islands men have vague misgivings because they have heard rumours of militant women overseas. That is true, but I have never met a militant Solomon Islands feminist and I don't believe I ever will.[160]

I was also affronted by a list circulating of dangerous taxis. Such a strategy did not seem to me to be fair or effective either for the public or taxi drivers:

> Some public action should be taken about the list of plate numbers of forbidden taxis which is currently circulating. The list alarms the public and may cause loss of business to innocent taxi drivers. It has been said that all taxi drivers should have a character reference stating they do not have court and driving offences and have not had previous traffic accidents. No other occupation requires such a character reference.
>
> It is in the interest of the public, and taxi owners, that drivers are reliable, safe and law abiding. Maybe taxi owners could form an association and vet their drivers.

A sticker could then be attached to the taxi so the public know they are in a safe taxi. If a driver commits an offence he could be prevented from being hired by any member of the association. If this scheme was successful women could even take taxis at night and feel safe.[161]

In November I finally covered a story which felt like a holiday rather than work. It was the opening of a tourist resort at Anuha. It was a perfect day and going over by boat we were accompanied by flying fish and dolphins:

> Anuha has come a long way since the night in March 1981 when Nikki O'Shea joined her husband Brendan under the Anuha 'Hilton', a tarpaulin stretched across a pole. As they lay underneath, a terrific storm raged and Nikki said they felt they were at the ends of the earth. Brendan O'Shea is a director of the new resort with fellow Australians Warren Howell and Peter Cornish.
>
> The opening of the million dollar resort two-and-a-half years later took place on a perfect day.
>
> The Minister of Finance, Bartholomew Ulufa'alu, opened the sixty bed resort and the guests were treated to an island feast.
>
> The three families led by Father Pule who own the land, have been involved in the construction. Fifteen basic cyclone proof sleeping units were provided by the Housing Authority and the locals were paid $900 a unit to provide a thick leaf roof and custom panels. They also

helped build the bar and restaurant with its 10,000 leaf panels, the largest wooden building in the Solomons.

The three local families have invested their lease money by building a supermarket in Tulagi which provides half the food used by the resort. They have also set up a cooperative store on the island. The first guests who arrived two weeks ago have already booked for next year.[162]

Sadly, five years later, in 1988, the resort was burnt down following a land dispute.

I also wrote about the first expatriate to be convicted of marijuana possession. He was found guilty and sentenced to three months' imprisonment:[163]

> A Honiara businessman, was convicted of the possession of marijuana and indecent videotapes on 28 November. He is currently on $500 bail as he has appealed to the High Court. Principal Magistrate Tony Parker sentenced him to three months' imprisonment and a fine of $150. The marijuana plants were found by Rove prisoners chopping wood on Mount Austen.
>
> His lawyer Andrew Nori said he had grown the plants as a substitute for alcohol consumption. He had been hospitalised in Central Hospital for seven days with an illness caused by alcohol and had also sought specialist medical treatment in Australia. He also said this was his first offence and he had cooperated with police.

In summing up Tony Parker said, 'There is at the present time, as far as I am aware, no drug problem in the Solomon Islands based on cannabis or similar drugs.

'This court will not stand by and witness the initial stages that could herald future problems. You know the taking of cannabis can be step one on the road to self-destruction and if it is made available to others, their destruction also.'

Tony Parker's concern about the possible spread of marijuana use has been justified. A 2018 survey by Dr Rex Maukera, Solomon Islands psychiatrist and an associate found that of 1411 high school students in Honiara, more than one quarter of them (28 per cent) were using marijuana.

Smoking prevalence was even higher at 33 per cent while more than a third of students (38 per cent) drank alcohol. The authors said this substance use has led to serious social, health, mental health, legal and academic problems.[164]

I also wrote constantly about public expenditure. On 8 December two stories jostled on the front page, one about Honiara town councillors granting themselves termination grants and the other about the increasing cost of national politicians' overseas trips:

> The Minister of Home Affairs Mr Kamilo Teke has refused requests by Honiara town council members to grant grand them each a tax-free $2850 terminal grant in advance. He said a terminal grant cannot be advanced

and is paid out at the end of the sitting member's term. He also said the town council is acting under the Local Government Act and there are no provisions in the Act for terminal grants. The total of these grants would be $34,200.[165]

Meanwhile, in the national government, the cost of MPs' and ministers' overseas trips had trebled:

> Ministers and Members of Parliament spent almost three times as much on overseas trips during 1983 as they did in 1982.
> During 1982, approximately $35,000 was spent. By December 1983, this had increased to $82,000.[166]

The government's priorities were evident in the budget estimates as I described to my parents in mid-December:

> I have been struggling with the budget estimates. Thirty new posts for police but no money to fund them. $18,000 so the Governor-general can maintain his private residence. More money for salaries for provincial staff in Makira (the Prime Minister's island) than anywhere else, although they have fewer staff than the larger provinces.
> Brian is now quite well again. George is looking after the children as we have no money for a house girl and he is also looking for jobs. We can't survive on the paper. He's sad.

Thank goodness it is Sunday. I'll write a few more letters, do some washing and then the children and I will go and fly the kite I bought in NZ.[167]

In January I wrote an article about Chief Justice Daly who was coming to the end of his contract. It provided the opportunity to include a simple description of the checks and balances needed in a transparent and equitable democracy. I believed people still didn't understand it:

> It is sad Mr Justice Daly is leaving. He has been a very fair and independent Chief Justice. I have appreciated his sense of humour, his sensitivity to the Solomon Islands situation and his championship of the ordinary person. It is unfortunate the government appears to be making little attempt to locate a lawyer of similar stature to replace him. An independent observer certainly has more confidence in a country where the judicial system shows an independent spirit and is prepared to take on the government when necessary.
>
> A democracy is a fragile and sensitive system which needs robust checks and balances. The parliament composed of elected members consists of the government and the opposition. The parliament makes laws and policy, and the government through its public servants ensures those laws and policies are carried out. The opposition watches critically and is prepared to take over if the majority of elected members support it.

The judicial system consisting of courts, lawyers and judges interprets the laws, tries those accused of breaking the law and sentences those found guilty. The media, composed of radios and newspapers is another important check. We are, or try to be, responsive to you. We probe the issues and ask the questions you would ask if you were able to. Lately the government has taken an ambiguous position to both the legal system and the media.

The Public Solicitor's Office, which provides legal services to those who can't afford private lawyers, is desperately understaffed with only two lawyers in Honiara. It is from the Public Solicitor's office that many of the court cases questioning government actions originate. It now appears the office will be permitted to recruit additional staff.

The media are also struggling. The radio received the same amount from the government this year, as last, despite their increased costs. As for the two independent newspapers, they have a daily battle for survival.[168]

I remember sitting under the tree on the bench outside our house as the sun was setting, I must have looked so sad. Brian, who was four, came and sat beside me and said, 'It's all right, mummy. We're going to be all right.'

It was Brian too, at the airport, who comforted John, who was crying inconsolably for his father. We were booked on a flight to Gizo in the Western Solomons where I was supposed to be covering a story.

It was a hard time, and George reflected on it recently in an article for Griffith University. He said my parents had bought land and built a building for the paper, and he took out a loan for a printing machine. While I, with my nose for news, helped as a journalist and Jane assisted with the advertising and administration, the effort needed to establish and sustain the business in such a challenging environment took its toll.

He said he was exhausted, and our marriage did not survive the journey. After we left in 1984, he kept the *Toktok* going for eight years until 1992 and then he rejoined the Solomon Broadcasting Corporation.

We did, however, leave a legacy with independent newspapers set up in Samoa, Tonga and Vanuatu following the *Toktok*. There was also a freelancer, NZ journalist Mike Field supporting the independence of the press in the Pacific. However, Mike was eventually banned from entering Tonga, Samoa and Fiji. George became his freelancer in the Solomons when he was the Pacific agent for Agence France-Presse.[169]

I wrote the piece below after I had left the Solomons in February 1984 and while I was still in Hong Kong with my parents:

My two children Brian, four, and John, two, and I, were waiting in a hot cargo shed in Gizo.

We were the last in the queue.

The passport officer was bewildered when I handed

him my passport and tickets. But he stamped the passport and handed it back. The airline official looked at the tickets and handed them back without tearing off the appropriate section.

My bags were in the terminal.

'Take them back to the plane,' I said. 'We're going on to Papua New Guinea.'

'She's going,' whispered one man to another.

We reboarded the small plane.

It was 7 February 1984. After almost seven years in the Solomons I was free.

As the plane flew over the bush covered islands, I looked down for signs of human habitation in the leaf houses, the villages that ninety per cent of the 200,000 inhabitants here, live in.

Seven years is a long time, I reflected, The first four as a nurse, the last three as a journalist on my husband's paper, the *Solomons Toktok*. Although a New Zealander I felt I had been absorbed into the life of the country as few other Europeans had.

I had changed, but so had the Solomons.

After independence in 1978 and the gradual severing of ties with the British, the Solomon Islands had worn democracy uneasily. There was so much political infighting in the capital Honiara where potential MPs jostled for 38 seats, and so much newly aroused nationalism together with embedded tribalism. In the village my husband's father, a chief, came up to me and asked, 'What is parliament? What do the politicians do?'

The 20,000 people in Honiara lived in a different world from the subsistence lifestyle of the rest of the country. In the villages they fished, tended their gardens of sweet potato, cassava, yams and taro, and sometimes sold copra made from coconuts. In Honiara, the Chinese, the public servants, the businessmen lived, and the gap in Melanesian society was widening. The wealthier tended to eat too much, drink too much, drive too fast and get coronary artery disease and diabetes. This was while labourers lived in one room with their six to eight children and wife and tried to survive on $SI 60 to $SI 80 a month or about A$ 20 by eating white rice and sometimes bush cabbage.

And me?

For the past three years I'd been in the thick of it as a journalist on one of the two independent newspapers while my husband George Atkin, was the Prime Minister, Solomon Mamaloni's cousin.

Our paper had a circulation of 2000, while our opposition, the *Solomon Star* boasted 3000. The radio, the Solomon Islands Broadcasting Corporation (SIBC), a statutory corporation, claimed an audience of 135,000. But despite our size, we were influential.

My marital situation had deteriorated, and I had grown to accept that it was almost impossible to operate an independent press in a developing country. The newspaper was not commercially viable, even if we purchased our own printing press. Events had come to a head after the previous three months.

I had been working in New Zealand and was about to take a brief holiday when I was advised by the office manager to get back to the Solomons. On arrival, I found my husband had quarrelled with the rest of the staff.

The only solution seemed to be that I continue producing the paper with the four other staff while he looked for work. It would have been impossible for George and me to produce it alone.

One of the first big stories broke in early November 1983. It dominated our front page on November 17 headed 'Price control in trouble.' The price control legislation had been introduced into Parliament during 1982 and it was assumed it had been passed and was now law. To enforce it, government officers regularly visited shops and wholesale outlets to ensure compliance. However, lawyers from the Public Solicitor's Office found that the Minister of Finance had not signed the Act. One local company decided to take legal action against the government for loss of profits. The government hastily passed retrospective legislation on 16 November 1983, legalising the Price Control Act from the time it had been assumed to be law.

In my story I outlined the form illegality of the Act saying, 'In theory this would make the government liable for compensation to businesses concerned, for lack of profits'.

It was this 'would' that got me into trouble.

I faced a contempt of court case on 27 January 1984 and was found guilty of prejudging a case before the High Court. Chief Justice Daly said in his judgement that inadvertent contempt had occurred due to ignorance of the law and inexperience. He ordered there be no penalty and no costs.

It had been the government who brought the case to court, and they directed that the defendant be representatives of the company who published the *Solomons Toktok*, News Limited, not the editor or the journalist who wrote the story.

The three directors of News Limited were George Atkin, Allan Taro, and Solomon Mamaloni, the Prime Minister. He had had been co-opted into this position before he came to power. So, when the government lawyer called for the imprisonment of the offenders, as he did, he was advocating that the Prime Minister be jailed.

I emerged from the case feeling rather shaky. I now understood how vulnerable my position was. The Prime Minister was legally responsible for my mistakes, and could if he chose, dictate editorial policy, although he never had.

I asked George to ask the Prime Minister to resign from his position as director.

However, instead Mamaloni declared he was not a director of News Limited through the opposition paper. This claim could have been disproved by anyone who went to look at the company's records in the Registrar of Company's office.

It was over the Christmas of 1983 that the Prime Minister went to Australia. He stayed away for six weeks and nobody, including senior cabinet ministers knew why he prolonged his visit and when he would be back. He had gone initially for medical treatment, although he had not been referred by Solomon Islands specialists. When the Solomon Islands public heard he had been discharged from hospital but chose to remain in Australia, speculation grew.

I wrote an editorial saying I felt it was irresponsible for a prime minister to leave their country without indicating when they would return. I managed to be at the airport when he did return. A week after his arrival we were at odds. He was now threatening to sue me because I made an incorrect statement saying he had sent his bill for medical expenses to the Ministry of Health who had not paid it.

He and his supporters paid his medical expenses. I responded by inserting an apology about that on the front page of the next issue. I then left.

Reflecting on my time in journalism in the Solomons I feel one area I influenced was that of women.

I took up the cause of a woman public servant who was to about to be dismissed. There seemed no reason for her dismissal, but she was in personal conflict with some of the men she worked with. Her expatriate employer said she could hardly be classed a firebrand, but then neither could most of her male work colleagues. I wrote a story and we continued to follow its progress. She was not dismissed.

Then there was the National Council of Women. This was a body formed in 1983 which was allocated a few thousand dollars in the 1983 budget. The women involved said there was barely enough to pay for salaries for two staff, and this left no money for touring. I questioned the Minister of Finance about the budget. In a later meeting with the council, I found the amount had suddenly and inexplicably been doubled, without a government press release advising of this.

In *The Sun*, February 1983, I wrote an article titled 'Wife beating is an offence' This included information about what help was available. On the same page Jully Sipolo, a well-known Solomon Islands poet and writer wrote the following 'Husband tosses wife around like a ball.' It was after this I was invited by the Solomon Islands YWCA to attend the National YWCA Conference on Rape and Domestic Violence in NZ in 1983.

I also wrote a story about a cabinet minister who was sentenced to jail for three months. (*Solomons Toktok*, February 3, 1983). He was released in March on the grounds of the prerogative of mercy and began to attend cabinet meetings.

It was one of the few times in the Solomons I witnessed a perceptible public reaction. People were angry. So, I spoke to one hundred people in the street with more than ninety saying that no one, including cabinet ministers, was above the law. They believed he should return to prison to complete his sentence.

Finally, the leader of the opposition, Sir Peter Kenilorea took the matter to the High Court, alleging that the Committee of Mercy did not have a quorum when that decision was made and so it was invalid. The High Court upheld this, and the cabinet minister returned to jail (*Solomons Toktok*, 14-21 April 1983).

In one of my last *Solomons Toktok*s (15 December 1983) as editor I wrote a warning about an increasing government budgetary shortfall, the narrow tax base, the cost of repaying debt as it burgeoned and the effect that imposing high import duties had on the cost of living.

I also pointed out the cost of maintaining a top heavy and inefficient public service, and the financial cost of not providing effective preventative and treatment programs for malaria. An example of public waste was the order for almost one million aspirins, presumably a mistake, and enough for fifty for each person.

The month before I left, I also wrote a series of articles on prison security.

I received information that an expatriate prisoner, who had been jailed for three months for growing marijuana, had been seen driving his van. His workshop was close to our office, so we staked him out, waiting on a nearby roof and took photos of him entering the workshop. The next week the photo was on the front page, titled 'Expatriate prisoner serving prison sentence'.

I found out he had been travelling backwards and forwards between the prison and his workshop carrying plastic bag machines so he could set up an ice block factory in the prison. Our story stopped this, and he was no longer able to leave the prison.

A week later the police got upset when the prisoners raided their police club, drinking large quantities of alcohol and stealing cartons of cigars. The police were very indignant about the prison officers who they said had not supervised the prisoners adequately. The breakout had occurred during a soccer match.

I wrote an editorial wondering whether there was any point having a law and a police force when the security of the ultimate deterrent, prison was so porous. We later found out and wrote that some of the prison warders had previous criminal convictions.

My series of stories and editorial finally began to have some effect.

The wife of the Australian High Commissioner complained that she had not been allowed to see the expatriate prisoner. He was permitted only one visitor and he preferred his wife. I managed to identify the committee which had been appointed by the Prime Minister the year before to look into prison affairs. The previous secretary had resigned after holding one meeting. The newly appointed secretary hastily began arranging another.

I also wrote about the finances of Guadalcanal province, the island on which Honiara was situated, being in turmoil towards the end of 1983. The province had simply run out of money. Suppliers would not allow them credit, there was no petrol available for touring and staff were not paid overtime and did not do it.

Apart from reporting the ensuing row between the provincial executive and the Minister of Finance I wondered what effect the shortage was having on services. I did a story about agriculture, but the most interesting story was about education.

I visited a school a few miles out of Honiara, which provincial officials said was not as disadvantaged as the rural schools. I found that five of the thirty standard six children could not read, so they would certainly fail the national test which would determine whether they could access high school, either a national high school or a provincial one. I visited the school library. There were very few books, even those in the syllabus were not available. This, together with the policy of allowing children to progress to the next class whatever their ability, and the high rates of absenteeism, were the reasons given by the teachers for poor literacy levels.

The greatest reward I received for my efforts, and I still remember this in 2020, was watching an old man reading a *Toktok* at a snack bar in Honiara. He was grimy and wearing only a loin cloth, and yet he was holding the *Toktok* with much reverence and reading it intently.

That is why I do it, I thought. That is what I am fighting for. This man and these people, deserve all the integrity, courage and enterprise that I and the rest of the media can give them.[170]

Chapter 8

BACK TO THE SOLOMONS WITH THE CHILDREN

We flew from the Solomons in February 1984 and stayed with my parents in Hong Kong for six weeks. My mother helped me settle the boys while my father flew to Wellington to prepare for our arrival. With the assistance of my cousin Stephen, he found a house near my aunt, his sister Eve.

It was a very hard time, one of the hardest in my life. I grieved for the Solomons, and so did my sons.

It was raining on the evening of 16 March 1984 when we finally settled into the eighty-year-old weatherboard house in Wellington and I wrote:

> When dad goes, comma I will be lonely, another battle. New Zealand is so strange. I look up the hillside and see those houses, all so isolated.[171]

The next day dad introduced me to Ping, my landlady's sister. Ping lived with her mother Mrs Yu and gave me cooking lessons, starting with rice. I was completely undomesticated. For seven years I hadn't cooked or done any housework. I was terrified of the washing machine.

The priority was the children. Neither of them could speak English and Brian was due to start school in mid-May. I had never looked after my children full time before and it was exhausting. John was drawing pictures of people with their heads cut off, while once I found Brian wandering on the road.

Four days later I wrote:

> John very upset, clinging and sad. Dad very tired this morning. I look at his mouth, it's like grandma's in old age, almost a death mask. He keeps on yawning. It will be a relief to see him go tomorrow. He will finally be able to relax.[172]

Things began to improve four days later. Writing to my parents, I thanked them for their support and reported John was smiling more and not crying so much. Both Brian and John enjoyed play centre and were beginning to play with the neighbouring children.[173]

By May I was working in the medical ward two days a week and Brian had started school. He had a supportive, kind, Maori teacher and enjoyed it. While I was at the hospital, they went to Maria's. Maria was a tall friendly Dutch woman who ran a homely day care centre for five or six children. She fed them from her vegetable garden and got a crate of milk each day.

In December 1984 I was accepted for the journalism course at Wellington Polytechnic where George had trained. On completion, I got a job with the *Independent Herald*, a community paper in Johnsonville, and bought a townhouse. A year later I began work as a public relations officer in the Ministry of Energy as we were struggling on my salary at the *Herald*.

In October 1986 my brother Peter, his wife Wendy, and two of their three children, Sam and Annabelle, were killed in a car accident in Hawkes Bay. It was devastating.

My parents decided they would retire to Australia and invited us to join them in Brisbane. We flew over in 1990 and settled in a small flat they had built next to their house in Cedar Creek Road. There was a creek and bush covered hills around us. The boys went to Samford School and became very popular as they were good at sport. After nursing for a year, I began an environmental health degree.

In December 1992, when the boys were thirteen and eleven, we went back to the Solomons. We arrived five days before Christmas and I wrote about the first, very long, night:

> Here I am writing on an airbed, the first light of day filtering through. There is a heavy smell of urine, and I can hear women and children chattering, while someone is chopping wood.
>
> I had forgotten how hot the Solomons is. As soon as we

arrived, we were jolted by the sauna-like heat. We waited in the shed-like airport for a long time. As we waited and more fortunate people left, I glimpsed George waving as the doors opened. Finally, we emerged and a driver from the Solomon Islands Broadcasting Corporation picked us up. The roads are terrible, full of potholes, and there is dust everywhere.

We passed the office at Ranadi which my parents funded and which has now been sold. We then dropped some cargo on the ship going to the village and went back to George's rented house. When we left, he insisted we sold our house although I was happy for him to stay there. He invested his half of the money in a fish and chip business which quickly collapsed.

This house is a concrete box like the houses in the labour line. The shower is slimy, the lavatory stained and smelly and the gas has run out. There is no light in one of the rooms. There are no mattresses and no mats. There is a fridge. The heat of the day is trapped by the walls and smites you at night.

I lay waiting for the faintest breeze from the propped open shutters. I had the best spot and then surrendered it to John who was tossing and turning incessantly. George and Brian slept in a neighbouring room. George is around 90 kg and my height, 160 cm. He lay on his back like a beached whale, began to rumble and then suddenly there was a volley of thunderous snores. John came over and begged for my earplugs.

In the morning we walked to the labour line to see Leslie Wate, George's brother, and his wife. Leslie stood unsteadily in front of his house trying to do up his buttons. It's strange how these people move me. He feels like a brother. He looks much older now, with a haggard, long, lined face and teeth stained red by betelnut. He is one of the hundred Solomon Islanders patrolling near Bougainville.

'It's dangerous. The Papua New Guinea troops are told to shoot to kill but luckily they are bad shots,' George said.[174]

This was confirmed by John Roughan, director of the Solomon Islands Development Trust writing in the *Solomons Voice* on 13 January 1993. He wrote that the Bougainville conflict which began in 1988 was a manmade horror with two Solomon Islands citizens recently shot by Papua New Guinea troops. He said the Papua New Guinea military patrolled the Shortland Islands as though it was their own territory although it belonged to the Solomons. He suggested the Solomons invite the United Nations Peacekeeping Force[175].

We took a minibus up to Naha to see George Ngeingari and his wife Martha from South Malaita. George is a cousin from South Malaita and lived with us at Vura. While George Atkin's living situation had worsened, George N's had improved. He was a senior technician at Telekom and lived with Martha and their three children and numerous relatives in a large house they had bought. There was a telephone, a fan, a comfortable lounge suite, and a big table.

We had a wonderful meal of baked kumara, fish, chicken wings and cassava pudding. Nason, our former houseboy, told us John was known as Pawpaw. This was because at the market he would stick his fingers into the ripe pawpaws and lick them which naturally upset the sellers.

After that first night John and I left for a rest house. After a good sleep I wrote:

> John woke up contented after twelve hours' sleep. It wasn't too hot, there weren't too many cockroaches, and the toilet didn't stink.
>
> Brian is resolutely sticking with his father. But it was John who refused to take the money George offered him, instead using his money given to him by his Grandma and Grandpa to buy his father a cassette player. He said he felt sorry for his dad who had a lot of cassettes and nothing to play them on. While the boys went with George to Skyline on a bus, I went to Chinatown. There I bumped into Father Abel. That meant more to me than anything. 'It's so good to see you back,' he said and put his hand on his heart.

'It's the same for me,' I said.

I went to see Ann Kengalu, a New Zealander, a former schoolteacher who had married Johnson Kengalu from

Ontong Java. I felt a failure and told her so. I compared myself and George with those I felt had made it, Alex and Telly Bartlett with their thriving hot bread business and George and Martha with their big house and George's stable job at Telekom.

Ann said, 'But you've got happy lively children and you always had so much courage.'

She felt that in terms of independent media, George and I had planted the seed.

As for the Solomons, she said, 'The economics is shoddy, corruption is rife, but the energy and life here are unstoppable.'

She said too that the SIBS reporting had improved dramatically since George had joined. I told her George said he had to give up the *Toktok* after a new magazine, the *Solomon Voice,* was formed. His staff left him and joined it.

Ann told me that Johnson was in the prison farm after being convicted of having petrol on the boat with his children when they sailed to Ontong Java. Ann filled me in on the politics and the expatriates married to Solomon Islanders. She said Mamaloni was corrupt and inscrutable.

One hundred Chinese from mainland China had bought passports and disappeared as had a hundred Malaysians. There was an industrial dispute with twenty-seven local doctors, many of whom had resigned and set up private clinics. Meanwhile, many patients went over to the Seventh Day Adventist Hospital at Atoifi in Malaita.

Those expatriates married to Solomon Islanders were tutoring those who wanted their children to have an international qualification rather than the Solomon Islands School Certificate.

Ann said that George went to Club 88, a casino. I told her I knew this as he had told me. George reported he had seen Mamaloni there recently. Mamaloni had given him some money, telling him 'To buy himself some more clothes and look smart for your wife.'[176]

Later I found that while George was the president of the Media Association, he organised a two-week course for journalists run by Nicola Baird, a journalist at the Solomon Islands Development Trust. Duran Angiki, one of the journalists who attended, said it boosted their confidence and he and Dorothy Wickham were subsequently awarded New Zealand scholarships.[177]

We flew to Kirakira the next day in a small plane John described as a ten-seater and about five metres long:

> The fattest person (my father) had to sit up front. The trip was bumpy but like Paradise. Mostly we flew above the clouds, but near Kirakira dropping below the clouds, we saw eight dolphins. The flight took two hours and we landed on the grass-and-dirt airstrip.[178]

We met Barnabas and at 3 pm left Kirakira for Tawatana in a fibreglass canoe with a concrete water seal toilet. I wrote:

Chapter 8 Back to the Solomons with the children

We arrived about 8 pm in tumultuous surf.

There were glimpses of familiar faces as they pulled the boat up the steep gravel incline. We were wet and cold. There were people pressing in, shaking hands, while our bags were carried up the hill[179].

Brian described meeting Basil:

As we were in my grandparents' house and I was shaking my grandfather's hand he was overcome by emotion. It was a very sad feeling.

But the next day was paradise. I woke up, ate breakfast, played soccer had lunch, played soccer, had dinner. Went to bed. What a day![180]

The boys were fascinated by their paternal great-grandmother, Kaha, now in her nineties. She had finally had a cataract operation and bulky glasses replaced her own opaque lenses. She walked with a stout stick, always had a pipe in her mouth and carried her tobacco in a string bag. She slept in a special bedroom with a fireplace as she got very cold.

I was so happy to be back at the Tawatana church for Christmas with Father Abel taking the service and the magnificent singing:

I have always loved this church with its open windows. You can look out at the trees, hear the sea and feel the breeze. Behind the altar with its crucifix are the woven panels of frigate birds and sharks.

After the three-hour church service, the conch shell blew and we all went down to the beach to wait for Santa Claus. I have never seen Santa Claus in a balaclava before. Neither have I seen him being paddled by warriors with blackened faces. Some of the older children felt his voice was suspiciously like that of retired police inspector Michael. Santa Claus gave each child a balloon and a sweet. There were great wails when the balloons burst as the children clearly thought they were permanent.[181]

John was more interested in the food:

> We had an island feast celebrating the birth of Christ and what a feast it was! We had pork, rice, sweet potato and many types of puddings. The feast was delicious. We should have more of these in Australia.[182]

After the feast there were speeches and Mr Ben, the headmaster, thanked us for dad's contribution after Cyclone Namu. They used the money to build a kindergarten. Afterwards there was custom dancing and I took part in a dance normally reserved for children.

All I had to do was stand up with two others when Manehau was mentioned, jiggle my hips and sit down again. There were cheers when we came off.

The other European, Michael Scott the anthropologist,

was more impressive although he did stand out with his white torso, glasses, and very red face and neck. While the others had white markings, Michael, appropriately, had black.

In anthropological terms Michael had a lot of catching up to do as there hadn't been an anthropologist in the area since Dr Charles Fox in the 1920s. But I found it irritating to be constantly compared with 'Scott' as the villagers called him.

Scott knew the language. Scott used the beach as the toilet and coconut husks as toilet paper, while we retreated to our water seal toilet with conventional toilet paper. Scott could eat six-month pudding without getting sick and do custom dances with the men of the village. He also had his own garden.

I explained that Scott had a six-month lead on me, and it was his job to learn the language and the custom. The women however were determined I would not be totally outclassed and I was to perform with them following a wedding the next day.

Brian said on Christmas night he felt sick, and it didn't help when carol singers from another village came after midnight and sang. However, he conceded they were great songs and great singers:

> I did nothing all day except lie down and read my *Mad* comic and *Sarum* and eat sugar cane and pineapple. John and Uncle Barnabas went diving. How I envied them.[183]

John described the 'rubber' they used while fishing:

> A rope was attached to the rubber. You put the unsharpened end of the metal into the loop of rope and pull the metal back. The rubber stretches and then you aim at the fish and let the metal rod go. We caught five reasonably sized fish this way and ate them for dinner with rice.[184]

The next day Brian was up again and he and John went diving with Barnabas. He saw a stingray and a parrot fish:

> John and I didn't catch anything, and Barnabas caught the most. We got home and we had a great dinner. I am not being sarcastic. Eunice, Barnabas's wife is a very good cook and we are eating like kings. We ate some of the fish and crayfish he caught. I love this village with its towering coconut palms and mangoes.[185]

The boys and Barnabas planted two coconuts just below Barnabas' and Eunice's hut as is the custom. They are usually planted straight after the baby's birth with the mother's placenta buried underneath.

It was Father Abel who had first told me about Sahu, and he added a sequel:

> After leaving Kirakira Sahu was second in command on a ship. The European captain was hated. He often ordered men to be beaten for little or no reason.

Chapter 8   Back to the Solomons with the children

Sahu plotted his death and, when he was diving, he was killed with an axe. The administrator ordered a punitive raid be carried out on the nearest village, and trusted Sahu to lead it.

Sahu led the party up into the bush. They let off a few shots, killed a few birds and set fire to a few old houses. Sahu then reported to the administrator that the village had been razed and all the inhabitants were dead.

Sahu developed the Marou Bay Plantation under Mr Campbell's direction and later married an Ubuna woman.[186]

I asked Father Abel about a cannon ball from Ubuna that Casper had showed me years before. He said that was the consequence of a raid by people from Gela. They had been defeated, but a couple of people escaped and alerted the authorities.

A warship was sent and fired on Ubuna. The villagers had been warned and watched from the hills as a few pigs and dogs were killed.

We went with George to see Haruta's garden on 30 December. John was impressed, writing:

> It is one of the best gardens in the Solomons and he doesn't even use fertiliser.[187]

I wrote:

His betel nut plantation was laid out in rows and was a money earner. Because of the drought he could sell three nuts for ten cents. Panas, a root crop which look like potatoes but are much nicer, were carefully staked out, as were the yams. Corn was planted in rows behind them. He couldn't grow taros because of taro beetles, while his melons had fruit fly.

Haruta's wife is old now. She is a widow whose children are grown up. She put down a mat and we sat down, me with John on my knee. Haruta laughed at him and said he would break it.

There is one small plump child wearing a porpoise teeth necklace and little else.

Haruta said grimly, 'He doesn't do what he is told, he has his own mind.'

They used to have a lot of children living with them. One by one they left, disenchanted by hard work and discipline.[188]

Later that day Brian was injured:

In the afternoon I was playing soccer with some boys aged between fourteen and twenty-five.

I was a forward and their keeper was a relative about eighteen years old. I ran to the ball; I can't remember how, but he kicked me when my foot was in a toe punt position. I could have sworn my whole foot was broken.[189]

Chapter 8 Back to the Solomons with the children

We learnt when we returned to Australia that his toe had been broken.

Brian described New Year's Eve:

> In the evening we went to eat at Stephen and Ida's house. Ida is one of dad's sisters and dad has eight siblings altogether. The food was very nice, chicken, kumara, pineapple. People were getting drunk on home brewed beer. At midnight there was choral singing, and it was hard to get to sleep.[190]

On New Year's Day we all went to Haurahu. While George and I stayed by the sea, the boys went up the river to make a dam. I went for a swim:

> It was very peaceful although the sea was rough. A cyclone was predicted to reach Rennell and Bellona at 5 pm. There were dozens of striped fish swimming around me.
>
> By 4 pm we could feel the edge of the cyclone, with thundering seas and an odd yellowish light. Haze and dust blocked the sun and white clouds skidded swiftly across the sky. There are two radios in this village of seven-hundred people and one of the schoolteachers provided constant bulletins about the progress of this cyclone, called Nina.[191]
>
> The cyclone passed over the village at 11 that night. People had readied their leaf roofs, placing extra leaf

and poles on them, and battened things down. We slept in a large barn, under a corrugated roof.

That night, there were great gusts of wind, and squalls of rain. In every house people were up. It was one of the few times I have been cold in the Solomons.

In the morning, when I went to the lavatory, there were fronds down everywhere. There were also a few damaged rooves and scores of unripe mangoes and bananas on the ground.[192]

The damage on the other side of the island was much worse. Sometimes during the following weeks we heard and saw army planes and helicopters flying overhead, presumably making reconnaissance trips and taking relief supplies.

We heard Nina devastated Rennell and Bellona and affected five provinces. Five people were dead. South Malaita and West Are (Malaita) were hit by a tidal wave, and houses on the weather coast of Guadalcanal were washed away. My parents must have been worried.

Undeterred, the Tawatana women's soccer teams kept to schedule and walked to Heuru for the games. We wore a hibiscus behind either the right or left ear which showed our availability. I didn't record which ear I chose.

Brian, our coach, described the match:

Mum was in the B team which lost 1-nil. Mum was the goalkeeper. They play seven minutes a half. It was nil all after both halves, so they played seven minutes extra time in which Heuru scored one goal.[193]

My recollection was:

> I did a header and kicked the ball a few times. I was a bit confused as to who was on our side. I thought we'd done well considering the other side had been training for weeks and we just turned up.[194]

The next day we helped clean up after the cyclone and then went to see Uncle Hoa, Rebi's brother in Ubuna. Brian was not impressed with that village:

> It is a very large village, and a place where even the ugliest person would find a couple of teenage girls.[195]

I was somewhat alarmed by a pack of Ubuna girls who followed us back, at a distance, occasionally stopping to giggle.

We were back in Ubuna three days later, this time visiting Pepertua, George's oldest sister and her husband John:

> Pepertua was afraid of wild bulls and cows in the bush, strays from a previous failed cattle project. They trampled people's gardens and one beast had been shot and the meat distributed. I helped with the cooking and ate some

of it. After this, I was up all night with vomiting and diarrhoea and had a yellow bucket. George was a great help, emptying the bucket in the sea, getting me water and putting the boys to bed.[196]

On Sunday, the big day came for the return match between Heuru and Tawatana, this time on home ground. Many spectators attended Brian, one of our coaches reported, not so much to support us but laugh and whistle at us. He noted the first teams drew one-all, but we lost two nil and I was the goalkeeper:

> It was traumatic. At the critical moment my defenders had disappeared, and their attackers got the ball through, hard, low kicks, just inside the corners.[197]

I recovered some of my dignity by assisting with a delivery the next day:

> Eunice came to me in the evening. 'Margie a funny thing has happened. A woman has given birth in the village. Harry Ramo wants you to cut the cord.'
>
> I followed her down. There was a woman in a small dark dirt hut. I could see by my torch that the baby was lying on the ground and the woman's placenta was still partly in. I picked up the baby and put him on his mother's breast. The baby sucked for a long time. Then

I asked the woman to push very gently. She did. The placenta came out and looked complete.

I asked them to boil my scissors, tied the cord in two places with string and cut it. We boiled more water, washed the baby and then the mother and put the baby on her breast again. As she suckled the mother expelled another clot. She was given Milo and biscuits.

George named the baby Brian John Atkin and we sent down a towel and soap. It was good to see the mother later that day looking well and happy, the baby wrapped in a towel. The nurse from the clinic came to see her and said everything was okay. I spoke with the women about not leaving a newborn on the floor but giving them to the mother to feed. Barnabas said before the clinic came the women knew what to do, but now they had lost their confidence.[198]

Two days later we had a picnic at night along past Haurahu and I wrote:

There was rice, kumara, chicken stew and cabbage and we were beside the thunderous sea, the moon partly obscured by clouds. The moon was orange.[199]

John wrote:

We came back along the seashore with lit palm fronds,

the embers blowing behind. Coconuts were silhouetted as was the eerie shaped rock with the skulls on top.[200]

He was becoming confident and like Brian, it was harder to track him down:

> The boys grew wilder as they went fishing, surfing with balsa boards, diving or shooting flying foxes with slings or bows and arrows.[201]

I also reflected on our time here and the change I had noted after twelve years' absence:

> There is a road now, but very little transport. Instead, there is the constant buzz of canoes along the coast.
> The cattle project failed and there is a transport problem with cacao and copra rotting awaiting shipment to Honiara. Conversely there is a constant shortage of goods in the small shops here, including sometimes, batteries and matches.
> Malaria and yaws are flourishing as are fire ants and fruit fly. Happily logging has not yet made it here.

Mamaloni, while he was alive, protected this part of Arosi:

> Slowly development is gathering pace. There are plans for the village school to be extended from standard six to Form Three.

There was also a women's literacy project supported by the bible translation team who are translating the bible into Arosi.

The first two permanent houses have been built and there is a stack of pipes and coil of hose ready for a water project. Many children have been born during my absence although some women now had a tubal ligation after their fifth or sixth child. There was a bank agency, but it was closed after the villager who ran it was jailed for misappropriating money.[202]

George and I had talked about our relationship so I was ready when Father Abel and Agnes asked me about it:

I told Father Abel I had no desire to be married to George again and was happy if he remarried. I said George and I had agreed that even if he did, the boys and I would always be welcome back to the village.

Father Abel said, 'Well, if it's like that, both of you should be able to get remarried again and you could even come back with your new husband.'

They were concerned a new husband might not think about the children. I said that I would never marry someone who could not think about my children. I would never desert them.

Agnes said I must always feel I could come back to the village and that I have my own friends here. She said the children are rich as they have two cultures.

Father Abel said how people in the village thought about people and who they were, not about how rich they were or what they owned.[203]

Later I spoke with George about my conversation with Father Abel and Agnes. He said when people asked him he told them that he loved and respected me, but there was no sexual attraction. I reiterated that I was happy for him to marry again. He said he had a woman friend but she was gay:

> At last, I feel George and I have worked ourselves out. I was looking up at the stars last night and I felt I was right when I told some casual acquaintances that I didn't regret anything. I'm very happy to have married here, and very happy to have my children. I am very happy to have had such richness of life and experience. Perhaps it isn't conventional but if people can't understand it that doesn't matter.
>
> When I told Agnes, it was possible I would never marry again she was surprised and said, 'They don't have women like that in this village.'[204]

Friday was the last day and the boys prepared by making lethal arrows:

> We went to make lots of arrows from sago palm leaves for Australia at Haurahu. In the afternoon I went skiing with John. The waves were not so big, but we had great

fun. At night we sat with John and lots of other boys and adults on Uncle Billy's veranda.[205]

Leaving the village I had a physical sense of pain:

> There were so many people down at the canoe in the early morning to say goodbye, Kaha, Rebi and Basil, Old George, Ester and George, Pepertua and her husband John, Charlie, Ben and Casper. Basil looked as though he would cry again.
>
> The sea was quite flat. It was quite extraordinary, the first calm since the cyclone. We drew out of Tawatana, past Mabel's house.
>
> I thought about 'The water of life', the words carved above Casper's door. I have learnt so much about myself and other people there. It's hard to describe. In that place, I realise who I am and what I have become. I understand what really matters and what doesn't.[206]

Brian also described leaving:

> This morning we left Tawatana. I was feeling very sad but felt better knowing I might come back for one year between leaving Grade 12 and starting university.
>
> The sea trip back in the canoe with Abel was calm for the first three hours but then it got rough just half an hour before we got to Kirakira. Every wave whipped saltwater

on to your body, but we were moving slowly and steadily towards Kirakira.

Kirakira is even worse than Ubuna. There is nothing to do here. Luckily, we only stayed one night in the rest house. There is a water storage tower here, but the rest house had no water.[207]

Brian then wrote:

This morning we got the small 10-seater plan back to Honiara. We saw Tawatana and Ubuni and Haurahu from the plane windows. It was sad.

Brian's farewell:

We have not done much in Honiara today. Mum and John are staying in the same rest house in the same room and dad and I are in the house. It is evening now, and I have to shower and put my mosquito repellent on and then have dinner. The others have finished dinner and they are still in the dining room. Good night![208]

On the flight back to Brisbane John said we should call Cedar Creek 'Tawatana' and that's what we did.

Jane and I on motorbike during *Toktok* days.

John, Brian and I in our yard.

The plane we flew to Kirakira in, in 1992.

Xmas 1992 and the arrival of the warriors with balloons and sweets. Barnabas supervising and Michael Scott recording.

Brian enjoying a feast in 1992.

Barnabas, the boy's great-uncle with his sons,
and Brian and John in 1992.

Haruta, the boy's maternal great-uncle,
and his garden in 1992.

Haruta's relative.
He had 'his own
mind'.

Eunice, Barnabas's wife, and the boy's great-aunt, with their children in 1992.

Basil with glasses, and a friend in 1992.

My good friend Ester, Rebi, and a friend in 1992.

Kaha, George's paternal grandmother, with her cataract glasses 1992.

Arrival back in Brisbane in early 1993
with the bows and arrows.

Brian and George arriving in Tawatana
by boat in December 1998.

George and Brian and family at picnic in Tawatana, 1998.

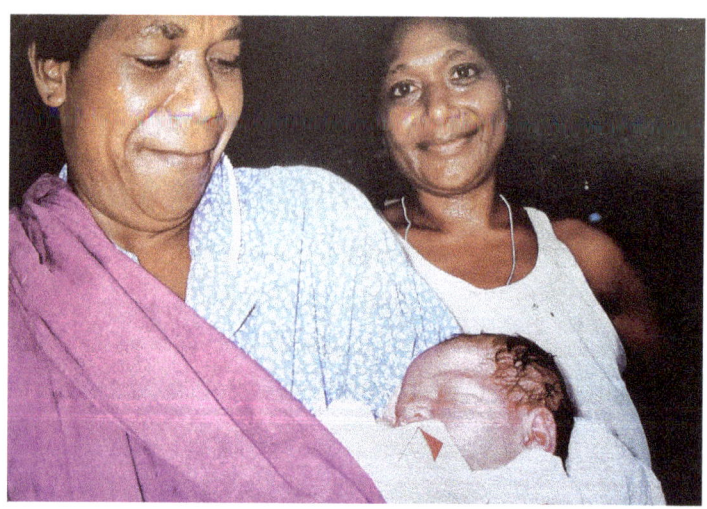

Ester with Nunuau and Nunuau's baby.

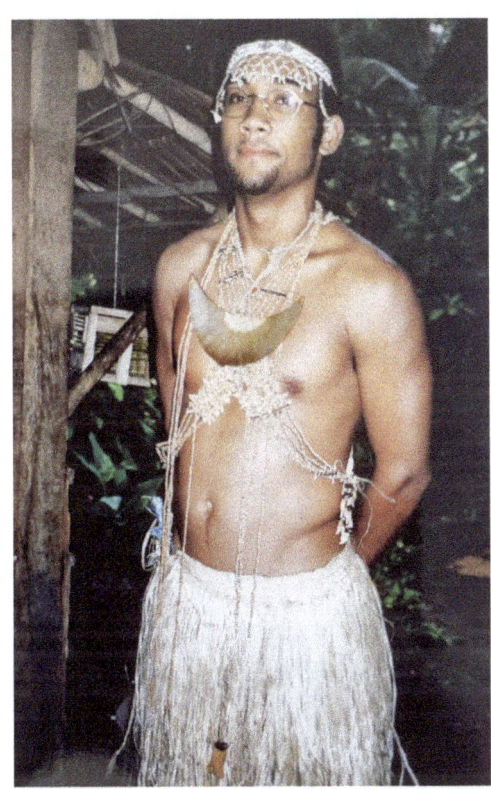

Brian in full custom dress ready for Xmas celebrations in Tawatana 1998.

Eunice holding a literacy class in 1998.

Brian and Meredith at their house in Tawatana in 2004. George now lives there.

Brian and Meredith's church wedding in Tawatana in 2004.

Cutting the cake Tawatana style 2004.

Wedding celebrations 2004, note the frigate birds.

Tawatana children in 2004.

Brian and Abeline, (Father Abel and Agnes daughter) in 2004. They were born in the same month.

Chapter 9

CERVICAL CANCER – A PILOT STUDY

I returned to the Solomons in December 1998. Pepertua, George's elder sister, had died of cervical cancer in 1997 at the age of 44. She was two years older than I. She left behind a husband and children, and I reflected on the injustice of it. If she had been an Australian woman she would have lived. Her two-yearly PAP smear result would have identified the pre-cancerous cells called CIN and she would have had these out, as I had done.

I wanted to know what cervical cancer screening program the Solomons had and whether it could be improved. I was doing a Master of Applied Science (Health Promotion) and chose this topic. Globally cervical cancer has been identified as the most preventable major form of cancer.[209]

Brian flew with me to the Solomons. He was nineteen and having a difficult time finding his life path. He enrolled in engineering at the University of Queensland, did not enjoy it and failed. He then worked with a friend, repairing and providing computers to the disabled, and enjoyed this. Following this visit he went on to complete a TAFE computer diploma and then an IT degree.

I spent the first two weeks in Honiara interviewing twenty stakeholders, including the obstetrician/gynecologist, the pathologist, diplomats, WHO officials, senior nurses and bureaucrats. I was given permission to look through the health department records. I then took a boat to Kirakira and found there was no doctor so I spoke with nursing and health education staff. Finally I was dropped by canoe at Wango and walked down the coast to Tawatana, calling in at the clinics. I kept a diary at the time.

Masey, the enrolled nurse at Wango clinic, told me she had not seen any woman with abnormal vaginal bleeding. She said family planning use had fallen dramatically because there was a rumour the most widely used contraceptive, the three-monthly Depo-Provera injection, caused cervical cancer. Masey said she was afraid to talk to with more than a few people at once, so half an hour later I found myself addressing a hastily gathered group of women and men. It was ominous that there were so few questions.

I slept at Wango and was accompanied by a nursing student. We continued to Aringana clinic where we stayed overnight before walking to Tawatana. George and Brian were due to arrive by boat that afternoon. As we drew closer I recognised the turns in the track, the rocks and the huts. Then we came upon them - Basil, George's father, and his brothers. They were brushing or clearing the grass from the track with machetes. Basil looked older and as he shook my hand a single tear coursed down his cheek.

Up at the hut where we had stayed with Eunice and Barnabas, the young girls of six years ago had grown into young women. One cousin was married and suckling her newborn. We sat in the shade of the big leaf verandah. Inside I could see debris from the boat which had sunk. After his first boat sank uninsured on its maiden voyage, he had found another and was still repairing it at Tulagi but was expected home for Christmas. Eunice had tried to call him that day on the solar powered church radio but was unable to because it was grey.

In the afternoon we went down to the beach to wait for the *Ocean Express*. It was windy and the boat arrived, but we had no petrol to send a canoe out to fetch the passengers.

We waited helplessly watching the flat-bottom ship rolling on the rough sea. Finally, eight men threw themselves into a boat and paddled furiously through the surf. There was a white woman and her small child in their first trip back.

They bobbed up and down just beyond the breakers. Then there was a furious shout from the shore, the boat caught a wave and crested in. Dozens of people surrounded it and carried it to higher ground. It was quickly unloaded while the American woman sat there, her head in her hands.

George and Brian came ashore next with deadpan faces. After a great deal of hand shaking, Brian turned to me and said, 'That's it. Next time I'm flying.'

For the next two days the sea raged, and the village was cut off. The American's husband was dropped further up the coast and I passed him striding purposefully with his pack.

George gave me a huge pile of washing. Down at the stream he also told me this was the first time he had washed in six weeks. His housing conditions in Honiara were not congenial. I'd discovered ten days earlier that he was sleeping on the table in his office next to Honiara market. It was very noisy with trucks arriving at all hours. The market was convenient because fruit was one of the few items he could afford. He was paid, but not regularly. There was a dirty toilet and a tap, which sometimes worked and sometimes didn't. He was producing a newspaper.

After a couple of days in the hut, Brian agreed to an outing to Haurahu, the small bay where we had picnicked and fished previously. There was now a hut there occupied by a Pileni woman from Temotu province, her husband who was from Makira, and their ten children. She was a passionate fisherwoman.

Brian became friends with their eldest son, Jeremy. They fished together, sailed in canoes and surfed on sago palm boards.

Brian was obsessed with catching coconut crabs and spent hours lighting fires in rock crevices trying to smoke them out. A small crab was given to us to be fattened but was eaten by mitomito, or fire ants, a most unfortunate end.

I saw Ester and talked with her daughter Rosa, a

beautiful woman who was a nun. Rosa spoke of the increasing number of street kids in Honiara, the product of family breakdown. At Church House they fed and educated them.

As we were talking, there was suddenly a tremendous yowl from behind the hut. There was a distorted angry face, a skinny naked male form and a torrent of unintelligible sound. He moved in the dust of the ground using his palms and his bottom, with his sticklike legs in front of him. Ester put a sweet potato in his mouth, but he spat it out angrily. She said he was cross because she had not fed him earlier. We hoisted him up, still squalling, one on either side, and took him back to his parents.

His name was Felix and he was eighteen, although he looked about ten. He was the youngest in a big family and his parents had never had much time for him. During the drought of the previous year, he got very sick, probably because he didn't get enough food. The others survived on Hong Kong taro and bananas. I suggested Felix should have some clothing and Ester agreed. We decided to walk to Ubuna as there was nothing in the local shops. A pyramid scheme had devastated the local economy.

That night I went to see Ida, George's sister and her husband Stephen. Ida was pregnant again. I reminded her, perhaps tactlessly, that she had planned to have five children. She was now heavily pregnant with her sixth.

'Oh, it was a mistake,' she said. 'I tried to use natural family planning and got confused with the mucus.'

I looked at her, an enterprising intelligent woman with a kind, cooperative husband and wondered what hope anyone had of following the method. I learnt later that in many villages two women were recruited and paid by the Catholic Church to promote natural family planning. The next morning I learnt Ida had gone to Ubuna clinic late that night and given birth to a girl.

Ester appeared early in the morning with a pot of food for Ida and we set off. It was good to be walking behind Ester again. I enjoyed watching her neck, which had a life of its own, constantly shifting and adjusting to support the pot on her head. She was much more sure-footed than me, on her wide splayed feet, feet which had never known shoes.

It was grey and windy. I suggested Ida might like a pineapple from Haruta's garden and we called in. Haruta, like his sister Rebi, George's mother, was a tall, slender, reserved South Malaitan man, different from the stockier more gregarious Makira people.

His hut was set back from the road and in front was his huge garden. His face broke into a smile when he saw me. His wife was dead and the strings in his legs didn't work so well, so part of his garden had been abandoned. He stopped our conversation to pick up a lime from the heap beside him and threw it hard at a hen which had been scratching in the wrong place. The hen squawked and ran away.

'I don't like to use stones in case I kill them,' he said.

He was miserable and I was sorry. He had married a

widow with six grown up children later in life, and she was constantly packing her bag and threatening to return to them. I asked gently whether he had a pineapple for Ida and he went off to find one while we watched the frigate birds.

There were dozens of them with their forked tails wheeling and soaring on the air currents. Haruta came back with a pineapple muttering about the youths who stole them, and to distract him I asked about the frigate birds.

'They like the wind – the big wind,' he said. 'They don't live on the mainland, but on rocky offshore islands like Bio near Ugi.'

Ida was suckling the baby when we got to the clinic and while Ester went to do her shopping, I asked Ida about Pepertua. Ida told me that when Pepertua first got the bleeding she went to the clinic. They had given her a needle and sent her home. When she got bad, Eunice had insisted she went to Kirakira and from there she was referred to Honiara.

Ida went to Honiara to look after her and stayed with George until Pepertua was finally sent home to die. Ida was stranded as she had given her money to George and had to wait in Honiara for months until finally someone gave her the money for the boat.

Ester came back with an old acquaintance, Nunuau, who was still keen to find a white man. I was unable to help and was relieved when she left.

As we walked back Ester talked about Nunuau and Michael Scott, the Scottish anthropologist. Not only did he have to elude NunuauNunuauau, but an even more determined woman. On his last night this woman had come to his hut. He saw her and fled, afraid to go back. He spent all night talking with Ester and George.

When Michael arrived in the village Ester had fed him, looked after him when he was ill, and taken him to see Rebi who told him custom stories. Once Michael had asked Ester to go with him to his garden and Ester gently reminded him local custom decreed it was not possible.

Frustrated he said, 'If I had medicine to turn you into a man, I would give it to you.'

Ester thought this was very funny.

Besides the nurse at the clinic there was Orimae, a custom medicine healer. I came away from that visit reeling. I had finally found where the women with abnormal bleeding went. They didn't go to the clinics because they knew they wouldn't get treatment. Instead, they went to Orimae who had been treating them for the last ten years. One year she had seen more than three hundred women. She kept records. They had come from all over Makira and some had even travelled from Honiara. She knew about Pepertua but Pepertua had come too late. Women needed to come as soon as the bleeding started. Pepertua came when she had been bleeding for seven months.

The village women I interviewed believed in Orimae and her treatments. She treated high blood pressure too and that could be monitored. She told them that if they hadn't improved within three days they had to go to the clinic. She had learnt her skills from a priest in Ysabel, and still had her medicine blessed by the priest although she rarely went to church. Instead, she believed in the old ways, the presence of the spirit in each rock and tree.

I understood why women went to Orimae; the Solomon Islands health system was failing them in every aspect of detection, prevention and treatment.

The Solomons had a PAP smear program and the smears were sent to Brisbane to be read. I was given full access to the results and found there were many problems. Almost a hundred records had been lost in 1997 and 1998 when approximately six hundred tests had been sent annually. Of those that arrived in 1998, almost a quarter could not be read because the woman had a sexually transmitted infection when the smear was taken. Then when the results did come back the women could often not be found.

Despite this, twenty-two women in the Solomons were diagnosed with cervical cancer, seventeen of them at a late stage, in 1998, with many of them in their thirties and forties.[210] At that time the total female population was around 200,000. These women needed treatment but there were not enough doctors to provide it, as a 1996 Review of Health Services in the Solomon Islands pointed out.[211] Dr Quan, the only obstetrician/gynecologist in the country, was busy with obstetric emergencies.

As a comparison in Australia in 1996, the death rate

of women from cervical cancer was 2.9 per 100,000 women.[212] In the Solomon Islands, data from Family Planning New South Wales (FPNSW) stated that the cervical cancer mortality rate was 17.9 per 100,000 women, a sixfold increase.[213] Family Planning New South Wales has supported the Solomon Islands cervical cancer prevention and treatment program since 2015.[214]

Finally, it was almost Christmas. It was clear that Barnabas would not get back. Preparations had to be made as Father Christmas had visited Tawatana every year since our last visit six years ago. Unlike European Father Christmases, the Tawatana Father Christmas was unpredictable. One year he had become Mother Christmas and another time had come along with his wife. His transport also varied. Usually he was paddled by warriors in a canoe, but one year he had come by helicopter.

This year, we decided he would have a grandson, Brian, dressed in full custom dress and accompanied by chief Peter Peter Dauoma'a. The villagers were divided into different groups with some collecting cassava, kumara and coconuts to make puddings, while another group hunted pigs, another possums and one group fished.

A man in the fishing group caught a very large sailfish singlehanded from a small canoe. The pig hunting group had little luck, so some paid for pigs while I bought a large duck from Basil for $SI20.

Making traditional pudding was time consuming. First, large numbers of dry coconuts were scraped and the coconut flesh squeezed through muslin to extract the cream. The cassavas were then peeled and grated and wrung through a clean flourbag and the paste mixed with the coconut cream. This mixture was pummelled and paddled in very large wooden custom bowls, then wrapped in banana leaves and baked with hot stones. I then helped Ester decorate the church.

I enjoyed the Christmas service with the beautiful singing, but time must have passed slowly for the children. Finally, we went down to the beach to wait for Father Christmas. First to appear were Brian and Peter Peter Dauoma'a piped by the bamboo band. It was an immensely proud moment for me as Brian, tall and handsome in the traditional chief's outfit, walked to the sea.

It was only when we saw Father Christmas that we understood the critical role that Brian and Peter were to play. Father Christmas had a green face, a terrible leer, and one eye hanging out from a socket. There was a collective gasp of horror from the children, and they were thoroughly relieved when he got back into this canoe to go and terrify children in the rest of the Solomons. It was Brian and Peter who handed the children their sweets and a balloon, while Felix also got a lavalava or wraparound cloth.

Later, I asked the organisers about his macabre appearance and wondered if they had got confused with Halloween. No, they hadn't, they replied. They were tired of the children recognising Father Christmas. This time they thought they'd fix it.

We then crammed into the village hall for the feast and listened to the chief's address. Peter Dauoma spoke about the growing population, about the twenty-one children born in 1997 and the six hundred children already present. The expected population of Tawatana by 2000 was 1000.

This population pressure was expressed in the increasingly bitter and divisive land disputes. The gardens were now further away and some had to walk an hour to ninety minutes to get to them. Fish were also becoming scarcer and it was harder to catch them off the beach. Most people dived or fished from a canoe.

On Christmas night George and I were sitting on the verandah when we saw a firefly circling around our lamp. George was convinced the dead came back as fireflies and had been terrified when a firefly almost collided with his nose the previous evening. This firefly kept its distance.

'It must be grandma,' George said. Kaha had died.

'Or perhaps Pepertua,' I added.

'How nice they've come to spend Christmas with us,' George said.

When I woke on the last Sunday morning of our trip, I was told a woman in her forties, one of George's relatives, had died in Ubuna overnight. She had been profoundly depressed, had lived alone, and had neither eaten nor talked to anyone for some time. She had been depressed since the death of her husband eight years earlier.

George was really shaken. He had grown up with her and always thought of her as strong and healthy, although he had seen her in the last few weeks. He wanted me to come. After church we assembled and walked to Ubuna in single file.

Some people carried bags of kumara or bunches of bananas. It was a grey day with occasional rain. The sea was calm.

As we came to the hut where the woman died and where her body now lay, there was the sound of wailing. I caught sight of her father, an old man, great sorrow etched in his face.

I thought of my own father who had just buried one of his daughters and felt I understood a fraction of what he was feeling.

'I am very sorry,' I said, and gave him my hand.

The mourning rites continued for seven days.

The return to the Solomons was a time of sadness, not only because of those two deaths but because of another. Not only did I miss Pepertua, but also Anne K, my friend who had died of ovarian cancer during my absence.

Seeking solace, I went to see Orimae.

I asked her how she felt about death, about ancestors, dead friends and family.

'The dead are always with us,' she said.

'It is only we who do not see them.'

Chapter 10

THE 'TENSION' AND BRIAN AND MEREDITH'S WEDDING

While I was in Cambodia during 2000 and 2001 the Solomons was imploding. I was working in a border province during an AIDS epidemic when news filtered through to me. The ethnic violence, the 'Tension' or the 'Troubles' as it is known, occurred between 1998 and 2003 with around two-hundred people killed and more than 35,000 displaced.

The backdrop was the resentment felt by Guadalcanal people towards the emigrants from Malaita. They worked on the Guadalcanal Plains in the oil palm and rice plantations and in the Gold Ridge goldmine. There were many Malaitan police and public servants. There was also resentment towards Malaitan men who took Guadalcanal wives thereby gaining access to land through the matrilineal land system, while some bought customary land.[215]

Members of the Isatabu Freedom Movement (IFM), formed on the Weather Coast of Guadalcanal, began harassing Malaitans. In 1999, houses, businesses and plantations were burnt and 20,000 Malaitans returned to Malaita. By the end of 1998 an opposing Malaitan militant group, the Malaita Eagle Force (MEF) had formed in Honiara. Both groups were armed with weapons, many from the police. Checkpoints appeared in Honiara with only members of religious communities permitted to pass. The turning point for the Malaitans was 17 January 2000 when fifteen masked men seized thirty-four high-powered guns from the Auki armoury.

There were shootouts in Honiara, and finally on 5 June 2000 the Malaitan Eagles, supported by Malaitan police, seized control of the police armoury at Rove. They captured naval vessels in Honiara and placed the Prime Minister, Bartholomew Ulufa'alu, under house arrest.[216]

I received an email from AUSAID on June 21, 2000, from John Roughan, director of the Solomon Islands Development Trust.

He wrote:

Solomon Islands women are at it again. They just held a major gathering in St Barnabas' Cathedral which was transmitted by SIBC. Certainly, women's actions and interactions are making serious inroads into the male power structure.

This time last year, on 21 June 1999, women organised themselves into a Reconciliation and Peace Committee. The first act was to rein in General Rabuka's tendency to shoot from the lip. They reminded him to do his homework first before sounding off to the media. He didn't like it much but on his return from Malaita he refrained from making public statements without checking his facts first.

Last Monday morning, 12 June 2000, 70 to 80 women gathered at the YWCA to listen to Professor Ade Adefuye, the Commonwealth's permanent envoy to the Solomons who was sent to advise about the social unrest. He said that the stumbling block to current peace negotiations was the Malaita Eagles Military presence and their guns in Honiara. The women asked about the other side of the equation, the Isatabu Freedom fighters and the opportunists who were using the mayhem to pursue their illegal activities.

Professor Adefuye said the 200 to 300 police who were neither from Guadalcanal nor Malaita, should be able to bring the situation under control.

The women determined that very day to visit militants on both sides of the conflict, to bring them food and speak to them as mothers, sisters, wives and aunties which they did and continue to do on a daily basis.

Roughan said, however, that time was not on their side with the situation becoming increasingly desperate. Already overseas ships were bypassing Honiara, so there were no new food deliveries, and no fuel, which meant no power, no water, and no phone. Central Hospital was also running low on essential medicines.[217]

By 26 June 2000 Manasseh Sogavare had become Prime Minister, supported by the Malaitan Eagles. The coup was denounced by many countries, including Australia which sent a warship to evacuate its citizens.[218]

I was also sent a newspaper clipping from Associated Press in July 2000, with an article headlined 'Patients shot dead in hospital raid,' Three hooded gunmen shot two patients, members of the IFM, dead at close range.

On 2 August 2000, a ceasefire was negotiated culminating in the Townsville Peace Agreement on 15 October 2000.[219] In October 2000, the country was in dire straits. Eight thousand jobs had been lost and the mine at Gold Ridge had closed due to raids and roadblocks. Fishing exports were suspended after a raid on a Solomon Taiyo fishing vessel in July 2000 and even log exports fell by thirteen per cent.[220]

In early 2001, I was advised of a position for a community development officer in the Solomon Islands, under Oxfam, with an annual salary of $40,000. I had not finished my work in Cambodia, and I also felt it was unrealistic and dangerous.

An extensive job description required the successful applicant to support not only intergenerational and inter-ethnic reconciliation, but the participation of women in peacebuilding, protect them from violence, and support various education and health initiatives. The budget was $340,000 annually for two years.

On reflection it took more than a community development program to stabilise the Solomons.

It took the Regional Assistance Mission to the Solomon Islands (RAMSI) led by Australia and supported by other Pacific Nations. This was initially a military force of 2,200, followed by a sustained period of support by civilian advisers and $2.6 billion.[221]

On 21 March 2001 an article in the *Australian* by Mary-Louise O'Callaghan said the hospital had stopped feeding its patients because it had run out of money. The peace agreement brokered in Townsville was monitored by five teams mostly from Australia. Eight-hundred-and-fifty weapons had been surrendered, but the militants on both sides still had access to weapons and a further 179 had been stolen from the police armory. She said after five months the peace process had stalled and former prime minister Sir Peter Kenilorea agreed.[222]

George's letter was dated 7 May 2001. He said he couldn't email and couldn't fax, and so had written:

> I hoped to go home for Christmas but didn't have enough money. Things were tough for me last year after I lost my job with Radio Australia. I have now resumed filing stories for Radio Australia but have not yet been paid.
>
> The peace process is fragile. The government is broke, and donors are unwilling to help while guns were still in the community. The prerequisite for donor assistance

is peace and they will only target health, education, and security.

The government needs $US180 million to rebuild the economy and the infrastructure and international financial institutions are only prepared to loan $US120 million for three years before they consider helping with development projects.

Security at the Australian High Commission has been tightened after threats were made. The media adviser to the Peace Monitoring Group was recalled after his life was threatened.

The media have been targeted by police after they reported the police shelling villages on the Weather Coast of Guadalcanal using a patrol boat.

I still don't walk around much for security reasons. You can't believe it but the Prime Minister jogs around with heavily armed men behind him. Even armed men accompany the Minister of National Unity, Reconciliation and Peace.

Where I reside, firing of guns has just stopped, but gunfire continues at White River, Vura, Naha, and Panatina. This proves there are still too many guns in Honiara. More are in rural areas of Guadalcanal and Malatia. The peace processes which were brokered at Townsville are disappointing as disarmament is very slow indeed. We'll just have to hope things will return to normalcy soon. Thank goodness life in other provinces including Makira is peaceful.[223]

Later, George told me he was chased by the Malaitan Eagles and believed he would have been killed but for the intervention of Alex Bartlett, a South Malaitan and a distant relative.

In December 2001, elections were held and Sir Allan Kemakeza became prime minister. When $US25 million from the last of four Taiwanese loans arrived in the Solomons in September 2002, tensions ran high. The worst job was that of the permanent secretary in the Ministry of Finance. He was a New Zealander, Lloyd Powell. He said he had guns poked at him, knives pulled on him and many threats made to induce him to sign cheques, but so far he had avoided it. Finance Minister Laurie Chan resigned in December 2002 after being forced at gunpoint by police officers to sign a check for $SI 3.6 million for 'unpaid salaries.'[224]

The government was desperate and planned to dump toxic Taiwanese waste on Makira, but this contravened the Waigani Convention and did not happen.

Then they were also going to sell eighty per cent of the Solomon Islands Development Bank to Australian investors until the Central Bank stepped in. The most bizarre scheme was advocated by a convicted Bougainville man, Noah Musinku, who said he would take care of the government's debt using an unheard-of currency. Finally, 20,000 Solomon Islanders spent more than $SI250 each on a pyramid scheme called the Family Charities Fund which promised to pay them $SI1 million after two months.

The banks had to close briefly after they were besieged by angry victims.[225]

A highly respected police commissioner, Sir Frederick Soaki, was killed in Auki with the gunman, who had escaped from Rove Prison, going on to shoot two more men. On Malaita, a missionary was beheaded in May 2002. In the same month on the Weather Coast of Guadalcanal, Harold Keke killed six Melanesian Brothers who had arrived to negotiate peace, calling them spies. There were later found to be seven graves.[226]

In March 2003 I found George had become the press secretary for the Prime Minister. Allan Kemakeza was a wily old fellow from Savo, a small volcanic island, and George respected him. But the country was to buckle under the unending pressure from militants with guns for treasury money. George also wrote that he had been home to Tawatana for Christmas and had seen Rebi who talked a lot about us.

In June 2003 patrol boats supplying food and ammunition to joint operations forces looking for Harold Keke were captured by his forces. The villagers of Marasa, who allowed the boats to land were punished. Two men were murdered along with the village priest and ninety-seven houses burnt. Finally, the villagers escaped back to the bush. Parliament failed to sit through the first half of 2003 as there was no money and it was unsafe. It was a failed state.[227]

In June 2003, Allan Kemakeza requested military intervention and Australia agreed. On 24 July 2003 the first of thirteen RAAF Hercules planes arrived, heralding the beginning of RAMSI. The militants surrendered, guns were collected and war criminals such as Keke found, charged, sentenced and jailed. Finally, the jail was secured to ensure prisoners could not escape.

✼

Back in Australia, in Brisbane on 22 December 2003, Meredith and Brian got married at Cedar Creek. A fairytale wedding in the bush setting; with the sunset and the lights reflected in the dam, it was beautifully organised by Daphne and Roger Kahler, Meredith's parents. It even included a dance floor. Meredith was slender and beautiful in a sleek white gown, while Brian was very handsome.

Almost a year later, in December 2004, Brian and Meredith reaffirmed their vows in Tawatana, accompanied by me, Daphne and Roger.

We arrived on 16 December and the next day I met George who was still working as a press secretary for the Prime Minister. He told me there were now Australians in all the key ministries including Finance, Tax, Forestry and Customs. The government was beginning to pay its debts and the Solomon Islands Development Bank had collapsed. While the rice plantations on the Guadalcanal Plains had gone, the oil palm plantation was still intact and under new ownership. The Kahlers went to the war museum on the Guadalcanal Plains and saw the burnt huts of the Malaitans.

George said Leslie his brother and a policeman were at the armoury when it was raided. His life was in great danger and he had to hide. Finally, this year the police officers responsible were jailed and he was safe again.

We flew over to Kirakira and hired a canoe to Tawatana. There were signs of logging including roads and slips in the hills with great piles of logs awaiting collection. In one bay was a huge logging ship.

At Tawatana, we walked up to the house and met Basil. He dissolved into tears. Rebi died in 2003 and Brian came back to her funeral alone. I put my arms around him and said, 'We loved her very much'.

Barnabas had also died, and Eunice was living up in Kirakira with Alison's husband looking after her two children while Alison attended teacher's college in Honiara. However, Eunice came back to the village for Christmas.

Brian had sent money for a house to be built in the village but when we arrived it was not ready. We stayed in the rest house where the Bible interpreters had originally lived.

On the first day, Saturday, we saw two frigate birds flying over the spot at Haurahu that Rebi loved. I was so grateful to Rebi's brothers and Eunice's relative Ben that it remained unspoiled. Ben had stopped the logging companies using Haurahu as a log collection point and Rebi's brothers Haruta, Hoa and Alick stopped them putting a road along the beach. They were offered $150,000. They said the logging company could have offered them $1500,000 and they wouldn't have taken it. We walked down to Ubuna with Roger. He said one of the whole logs he saw would be worth $A300 in Australia.

It was a shock to see Hoa a few days later in his dark hut. He had always been a heavy man but now his face was grey and his belly rotund. His legs were swollen, red and shiny and he was breathless, so breathless he couldn't walk. He had congestive heart failure. Brian without knowing it had paid for a drum he used as a toilet. I whispered to George and asked him if it was appropriate to thank him. He said it was.

I held his hand and thanked him for saving the beach for the family and for the village. It was the last time I saw him. After we left Tawatana we heard he had died.

Haruta also looked much older. He had lost sensation in one half of his body but still walked with a stick. His garden was in bushes and his hut in ruins. He told us sadly his chickens were gone (an eagle ate them) and his betelnuts gone (children stole them). His 'grans' brought him food. He had managed to walk down to the village for Rebi's funeral but would not be able to walk down for Brian and Meredith's ceremony. That evening we sent him a large sack of rice and a bundle of leaf, which we hoped his grans would use to repair his roof.

Late one night sitting with Eunice we saw a firefly. Eunice told me that the fireflies seen in the dusk in the plantations were just fireflies but those you see late at night were the spirits of the dead welcoming you. Eunice said they did not have Father Christmas the year Barnabas died as he had begun it. To honour his memory they put balloons on his grave every year at Christmas

We went to the cemetery down by the sea where Barnabas, Rebi, Pepertua and Dorris were buried. Dorris, a retired nurse, and Dorris's sister, like Perpetua, had died of cervical cancer. I knew then that the human papilloma virus (HPV) was the cause of cervical cancer and that a vaccine was in the pipeline. I was determined to watch its progress.

On Sunday we went to a long church service of three hours. We listened to the magnificent singing and heard the marriage banns read out. The congregation was asked if anyone had any objection to the marriage of Brian and Meredith or to that of his cousin Rex and his fiancé Freda.

We moved into Brian's house three days before Christmas and that same day I went with Ester to her garden. It was a fine day and a beautiful view from the top.

I enjoyed speaking with her daughter Rosa who had been an Anglican sister for ten years. She had been sent back to the village to decide whether to take her final vows. She was a slender, elegant woman and told me she had fallen in love with a Catholic brother who was also on the verge of taking his final vows. As a sister, she had learnt about prayer and discipline and talked of stewardship of one's time, one's body and the environment. She had also done a lot of counselling.

Chapter 10 The 'Tension' and Brian and Meredith's wedding

Before Christmas I went with Roger and Billy into the bush to check the source of the village's water supply. Roger was determined to expand the water supply system to include the school. There were many leaks. He identified the major ones and decided to glue the pipes. Peter Adams, George's brother, was trained to repair and maintain the system and did so successfully for many years.

We got used to the daily round. When the church bell rang at six calling people to prayer we got up and had breakfast which included fresh bread and fruit. George approved as we were both tired of kumaras and bush cabbage in coconut milk twice a day. The women would wash their pots in the stream, and their clothes and lay them on the stones. Drinking water would be fetched from the spring and then many went to their bush gardens. In the evenings they cooked over their fires in the outside kitchens and bathed the children. Some men and younger people played soccer.

We were all busy in the days before Christmas. The women's role was easier, peeling sweet potatoes and helping make custom puddings, while the men were expected to kill the pigs. George, Brian and Roger agreed the way they did it was cruel. The pigs were cut up and each house allotted a pile of raw pork and peeled sweet potatoes to cook in a traditional oven.

I saw Ida, George's sister, who was pregnant again, look at her pile despairingly. Her two eldest daughters had disappeared. I helped her carry the potatoes and meat to her hut and stayed until her daughters returned from Ubuna.

Basil was worried that Fred, who lived in the bush, hadn't received his allotment so I carried it up with Billy and Phoebe, one of Eunice's daughters. It was pleasant walking up through the gardens in the evening. When Odi, Billy's wife, needed help, Roger volunteered.

That evening Brian began vomiting. Meredith, George and I sat with him in the gathering darkness. George thought Brian was upset because of the way the pigs were killed. Meredith thought he was exhausted from sitting up until midnight every night telling stories and getting up early the next day. Meredith gave him some Gastrolyte and slowly he got better. She said this had also happened during Rebi's funeral and he returned to Kowanyama sick and exhausted.

The Christmas church service was long and not very edifying. The village priest spent forty-five minutes talking about Satan dwelling in young people. This was because they spent their evenings drinking and playing cards and didn't come to church. Finally, we were released and went back to Eunice for a quick cup of tea before dressing.

Roger as Santa Claus put on a Santa mask, a pair of flame shorts and had a pillow tucked into his pants, while I was a red reindeer in a long red dress. Down we went. The large fibreglass canoe was decked out with balloons. There was giggling in the bushes and four women emerged in trousers and hats and sandshoes, one with a pair of binoculars. I asked if they would be fined by the village committee.

This constantly happened to me as I always wore trousers. Someone else paid the fine so I wouldn't be troubled by it. I was told in this instance it didn't count because they were doing it for fun.

Ben blew the conch shell, the canoe was launched, and the women warriors slowly paddled us around the point. We caught one of the waves and were carried ashore to be greeted by warriors with black spears. After a haka-like greeting we walked up to the trees where the choir sang a welcome song and Santa Claus responded.

It was a very moving moment for me. I thought back to my first arrival all those years ago, alone with George. I thought of the naked small children, how alien it seemed, and how alone I was. I thought of all those I had known and loved, Pepertua, Barnabas and Rebi and how we had become part of this community with our sons, their wives and families. We then got into the serious business of distributing lollies and rubber bands to the children. We also gave lollies to the adults, including Ida who ate for two.

The wedding was planned for Boxing Day and that night was hectic. Brian began vomiting again and there was a storm with heavy rain, lightning and thunder. It stopped as abruptly as it had started. Aram, the trainee priest and deacon sent a runner, wanting more details about Brian's life and six carol singers appeared. They sang two songs in English and I gave them bars of laundry soap.

In the middle of the night George appeared. They were baking the wedding cakes and needed some milk powder and sugar. By that time Brian and Meredith were asleep.

We were all up early. Brian had a frigate bird painted on his back and Meredith looked lovely in a simple white dress with shell jewellery on top. Their bridesmaids also wore custom dresses.

Rex wore a suit while Freda wore a white gown. She was tall, statuesque and proud. Her father was at the wedding but not her mother and sisters as the full bride price had not been paid.

We walked into the church, beautifully decorated with flowers and green and yellow grasses. There were five priests/deacons there.

All the relatives came, from Waimarae, from Ubuna and from Marou Bay. NunuauNunuauau was also there, the woman who had pleaded with me during my last visit to find her a white man. Happily, she didn't need one now. She had married a man from the Weather Coast five years ago, a good man, and she was happy.

Roger gave Meredith away while George went up with the ring and they remade their vows. Then Rex and Freda were married. Aram's sermon was in English and about the need for the couple to tune in with each other and grow to know each other before they had children. Following the sermon there was holy communion and. wonderful singing. The cake was cut and on the way out from church the newlyweds shook everyone's hand just as George and

I had, twenty-nine years earlier. Ester and I started to sing, *We love you just as you are*, accompanied by the crowd clapping.

The feast was magnificent. Billy said after he was proud of it as there was plenty of food to take away. After the feast the cake was shared around and there were speeches. There was dancing, men in their grass skirts with marked bodies, brandishing their clubs and flicking their fingers. The women danced, bare-breasted and proud, with rattles attached to their knuckles. They then went into the stream cupping the water with one hand and bringing their other up, making a noise between a boom and a clap. Out in the slightly choppy sea there was a large pod of dolphins gamboling. I hadn't seen them here before.

I rushed up to the house to take the food parcels to Haruta and Hoa. Eunice came with me. We walked smartly so we could get back before nightfall. Haruta was happy with the food but disconsolate about the leaf for his roof. His grans couldn't do it. The man who used to do it was now in prison. It was a problem for another day.

As we got to Ubuna and passed the clinic there was wailing. We stepped out of the way. A procession passed. A mother was carrying her dead son, only ten years old. He had died of malaria, shortly after they arrived at the clinic.

On 29 December the Kahlers left and George told me there had been a massive tsunami in Indonesia on Boxing Day. I learnt later it had killed 230,000 people.

On 31 December George and I walked down to Marou

Bay with Meredith and Brian. On New Year's Day I woke up at Tegu (George's sister) and her husband Francis's house. It was a lovely spot, his mother's land, overlooking the sea. When we arrived the day before we climbed down to a narrow ledge which dropped straight into the deep ocean and looked down to see the shadows of huge fish many metres below. No wonder it has been a harbour for hundreds of years. Francis said the sharks here were friendly and warned him if he was diving, if a 'rubbish shark' was around. We climbed back to the hut and got there as it began to rain. We sat looking over the Weather Coast as the evening and the rain fell. Not far away there was logging. This is limestone country, and some people believe there is an underground American army living in caves, ready when called to liberate the country.

George told us about the inland track through the bush that the dead followed to Marou Bay. There was an ancient tree which leaned over a tiny island. A canoe came for those who were good and they were taken to Marapa Island off Guadalcanal, an island of ghosts. George said the locals were terrified about going there. Those who were not good were condemned to wander forever in the Makira bush and haunt the living.

Tegu and Francis told us Edna, their daughter, had looked after Rebi when she was sick. One of their sons was helping repair Haruta's leaf roof, but he had been jailed. George said he had fallen out of a coconut on to his head at the age of fifteen and hadn't been right since.

On 4 January we went up to Kirakira in the canoe, accompanied by Basil. I set him up with a regular allowance from the bank and then he went back with the driver. On 6 January we flew back to Honiara. There had been some question about whether I was going to Sudan with MSF and I was relieved when they called it off a few days later.

George thanked me for the interest I had taken in the problems with logging and HIV/AIDs. I was concerned about the loggers, some of whom had come from Malaysia, about their underage 'wives' and the possibility they were spreading HIV. George said he would write a story about it. I finally flew out on 11 January and Brian and Meredith picked me up at Brisbane. They told me Roger had been hospitalised on his return and had IV antibiotics after a bruise turned into cellulitis. I was sorry to hear it.[228]

Chapter 11

CHINATOWN BURNS AND LOGGING IN TAWATANA

Little more than a year later, in April 2006, I was back in the Solomons. George's brother, Billy, was worried about the extensive logging around Tawatana and I was worried about the potential for an AIDS epidemic. Some of the loggers had worked in Papua New Guinea during an AIDS epidemic with 57,000 infected people.[229]

When I emerged with my pack from the Honiara terminal I did not know if I would be met. I had written to George but had had no acknowledgement. I was looking for a taxi when George, Kendrick, my former nursing school colleague, and his wife Alice greeted me.

'We couldn't let you loose around Honiara,' Kendrick said.

George had considered my proposal to walk up the Makira coast and talk to people about HIV. There would be people to accompany me he said, and Billy was looking forward to seeing me.

It was 7 April 2006 and I had a couple of working

days left before Easter. It was a treadmill. By the end I had booked a boat and air ticket, sent a service message by radio to Billy and spoken to with five different organisations including the Ministry of Health and the HIV/AIDS unit. I had obtained condoms, pamphlets and charts, spoken to environmental organisations including Greenpeace about logging, and begun assembling a list of supplies for the village.

It was a relief when Easter finally arrived. On Saturday morning George and I went shopping, buying bulk tinned fish, rice, kerosene, toilet paper and other necessities. While we were walking around Chinatown a big LandCruiser went past belonging to John Lemani, the editor of the *Solomons Star*.

They had been our main competitor thirty years ago but because of our financial mismanagement, they drew ahead. I left and George finally abandoned the paper to work with the government.

'I'm not jealous, I like the simple life,' George said. After the struggles we had with the newspaper, I believed him.

Kendrick and Alice spent Saturday with others in the Anglican cathedral decorating it with flowers. On Sunday we were early, and the service began when the Governor-general arrived. The last time I had been in the cathedral the sermon had been about the seven Melanesian brothers killed by Harold Keke when they went to him on a peace mission. One of them, a couple of weeks before he went, had a dream where a great wave had broken over him while he was on a beach. In his dream it had momentarily stunned, but not killed him.

This resurrection theme was taken up again in the Easter message, carried upwards by the pure and passionate singing and the accompanying throbbing of drums. An unending stream of people went up for communion. They came from the church, from the lawns, from the car park. Last were the children, the smallest in their mother's arms, queuing for a blessing.

After church there were two family gatherings, one with George's brother Leslie, and his wife and daughters. We dined on rice and tinned fish and hot cross buns, then rushed to Alice and Kendrick's for a more elaborate feast. There were many people from Isabel, and after eating mightily, they sang impromptu songs and danced, the men and the women separately, joking and laughing with each other. The men had the monopoly on the drink including the communion wine, but I cadged a beer.

Monday was another public holiday and Alice and I went to White River to see Rosalie Habu. Rosalie and Mostyn Habu had been great friends thirty years earlier. When I abruptly left the Solomons with my two sons, I sensed I was persona non grata, at least with Mostyn. But I was shocked to learn of Mostyn's death a couple of years earlier. He was in his early fifties and died from diabetes. Rosalie and I had a lot of catching up to do.

She greeted me from a crowded and well-worn room. There were three houses on the White River site inhabited by her sons' families, including some of her eleven grandchildren. Her grandchildren came and went throughout our stay, and three of her rather embarrassed sons were introduced.

A slight woman, Rosalie is now a matriarch. As we ate rice, noodles and fried luncheon meat, she told me their story. When Mostyn was diagnosed with diabetes the family changed their diet. However Mostyn began to get foot sores which would not heal. He was admitted to the hospital during the 'Tension' when staff were unpaid, and two gang members were murdered while they were inpatients.

He was there for months and finally asked Rosalie to join him. The doctors cut off one foot, and decided they needed to keep lopping off more of his leg. He was discharged, but then got sores on his other foot. The doctor advised him to have this leg amputated too, but he refused. Instead, he and Rosalie went to Isabel for a holiday and spent their time on the beach. She said she would never forget it, and the memories strengthened her for the days ahead. When they came back, Mostyn was at home a few days, and then died peacefully. Another of his siblings has also died of diabetes.

'Our men die young,' Rosalie said.

Thirty years ago, there were five European women married to Solomon Islanders. Three of these men are now dead, one is in prison and then there is George. He may not be flourishing financially but he is a survivor.

We went to visit George Ngaingeri and his wife Martha

in their large house at Naha. This suburb hadn't existed when we lived in Vura thirty years ago. Martha now ran a small shop underneath, which provided her with pocket money. The house was full of students and there was a feast laid out in the kitchen. They hadn't eaten much on Easter Sunday, saving the celebration for our visit. We rang George. He couldn't afford a taxi, so I told him I'd pay when he arrived. It was great to eat taro, fresh fish and baked kumara pudding. I was sad though. The previous day I'd walked to Vura and passed our old house. Unlike many others it had not been renovated and all the trees in the yard had been cut down.

Almost two weeks later on 20 April 2006 I was due to board a boat for Makira. I sent an email to my family telling them I was leaving. It was 2.30 pm but within half an hour all the shops had closed. There were crowds of people leaving work early to get back to their houses.

I squeezed through a partly open door in a shop in Chinatown. I was to board the boat in an hour and I suddenly realised I had nothing to eat for the sixteen-hour journey. The Chinese owner had a mobile to his ear and hastened towards me.

'Quickly,' he said.

I bought two oranges, biscuits and a tin of bully beef and he chased me out and locked the door.

Thankfully I had taken everything down to the ship that morning, but I had to get there myself. I walked to George's house on the other side of Chinatown.

We had agreed to meet there at 3 pm but he wasn't there. It wasn't surprising. As the Prime Minister's press secretary surely, he'd be locked up with the politicians in Parliament. They had announced the results of the election at midday, Snyder Rini from the ruling party had won and a crowd outside had thrown rocks at the parliament. We tried his mobile. No response.

'All right, but I must get down to the ship. It goes at 4 pm,' I said.

Alick volunteered to come down with me. A fit and sensible man in his fifties, Alick was Rebi, George's mother's, youngest brother. We walked down to the town centre and the wharf, against the general flow. All the shops were closed except for the hot bread shop, owned by Malaitans. The girls, looking dubious, had half closed the shutters.

Near the wharf there was a traffic jam and cars started to turn around. People milled around and there was the sound of a shot. Alick and I turned a corner and I glimpsed George.

'George,' I called, and when he came over, I asked in a softer voice, 'How did you get out?'

He didn't elaborate but said he had come to say goodbye. As we waited, we watched thick smoke billowing from burning vehicles on the hill below parliament. A military helicopter was circling. George told me there was looting around Point Cruz and the shot had been fired by RAMSI who had also used tear gas.

Later I heard on the ship that someone had looted

mattresses and loaded them on the ship beside us. RAMSI had come down in a van and taken them back again. Another looter had been besotted by images of Christ and taken nothing else.

George was reluctant to go back into the melee when I said goodbye. He was sorry not to be joining me on Makira. He asked for taxi money in case he had to get away quickly. I gave him money, wished him well and boarded the boat.

I had one small bed in a stuffy cabin loaded with other people's gear. I decided to sit outside on the back bench. We left the wharf and for the next two hours went round and round the harbour. It was almost dark when we left and at that stage, we could see the fire at Chinatown. As we sailed away it grew larger.

The Australian captain's wife contacted him and confirmed Chinatown was burning. Later we saw a Hercules flying over carrying Australian troops.

Arriving in Tawatana the next morning around ten, I heard no-one had died, although some had been injured jumping out of windows. One thousand Solomon Islanders had marched to Parliament House after Snyder Rini was elected. He was the Deputy Prime Minister in the former prime minister Allan Kemakeza's administration, and many felt the Chinese were given an unfair advantage in trade, logging and fishing. There was anger about the perception that Taiwanese businesses had funded the election.[230]

John Lemani of the *Solomon Star* said people watched

Chinese arrive and within two weeks they had buildings going up on prime sites. Visas and passports were also handed out without going through official channels. More than a thousand Chinese from Honiara were registered as displaced by the Red Cross with more than four-hundred housed in Honiara's main police station after losing everything.[231]

On 22 April, China chartered a jet to evacuate ninety Chinese and on 26 April Synder Rini resigned. Manasseh Sogavare became Prime Minister on 4 May 2006.[232]

When I arrived at the village, I was shocked by the damage and scale of the logging and wrote to my parents on 21 May 2006:

> The Tawatana Stream is dirty, the Ubuna Stream is dirty, and the Maranu'u stream has dried up. The Haurahu stream is the only one still running clear.
>
> It is at this stream that every morning the loggers from the Yankin Bayan Company drop their washing and their house girl. It is at this stream every afternoon that their utility drops the loggers for their evening wash.
>
> And hour after hour, day after day, the trucks continue to roll, hauling giant logs. Sometimes, as they roar along the dirt road belting down the hills and picking up speed for a steep climb, logs roll off. At HaurahuHaurahu, two logs lie alongside the road, and a further log has fallen off before the climb to the school. Luckily no-one has been hurt or killed. The trucks had previously worked day and night until a village delegation protested.

Chapter 11 Chinatown burns and logging in Tawatana

The logs are stacked at the log point, Sino Camp, they call it. A large overseas freighter called, and before it was loaded the point swarmed with log scalers, checking the cubic metres cut on behalf of the landowners. The landowners made $SI50 or $A10 a cubic metre from the logs. If they had sold them directly to buyers in Honiara, they would have made $SI1500 or thirty times as much.

Sino Camp is infamous for the violent and pornographic videos the Malaysians show the village youth. Some young girls are 'married' to them, and there are several light-coloured infants.

The story I liked best was about the logger whose Solomon Islands partner gave birth to a very dark baby.

'What did he think?' I asked.

'He thought it followed the mummy,' was the reply.[233]

Although the loggers had bulldozed sacred sites, damaged gardens, betelnut and sago palms and contaminated most of the streams the villagers accepted their presence, until they began to contaminate the Tawatana water supply.

The water supply was working well and had recently been extended to the school, thanks to Roger Kahler, Brian's father-in-law. Roger, an engineer, had visited the village and had been widely admired because of his energy, persistence and effectiveness. The village men accompanied him in shifts as he strode up to the dam, checked the tank, walked the pipelines, advised on leaks and measured the flow with buckets. It was found that innumerable leaks were causing low pressure. Village men were trained, materials sent from Honiara and the water system repaired.

It was this I alluded to when I addressed the Tawatana villagers after Sunday Service. I was supposed to be speaking about HIV/AIDS but Eunice and I decided I would speak about the water. Eunice had accompanied me on other village, school and clinic visits earlier. Eunice was a Mothers' Union leader, a literacy teacher and highly respected in the village.

The day before, Eunice had noticed the water in the taps was brown for the first time. There were reports that Haurahu had become muddy. The problem was the road the loggers were building high in the bush. I had been in the bush the day it had rained, the day the water had turned cloudy for the first time. I had seen for myself the devastation the logging had created and decided it was time to talk about it.

When the people gathered, I began, asking them in pidgin what they were doing.

Would they wait until the drinking water became completely contaminated?

Would they wait until their children became sick?

What would I tell Roger who had contributed so much?

Would I tell him they sat there while their water became progressively more polluted?

Eunice told me afterwards that plenty of people looked ashamed.

Chapter 11   Chinatown burns and logging in Tawatana

We discussed the strategy with Billy, Eunice and other leaders. Billy had formed a non-government organisation to address environmental concerns such as logging. There were twenty-eight people on the board and he had tried to call a meeting three days in a row but could not get a quorum.

'Why don't the women and children march down to see the licensee,' I said. 'And hand him a petition about the water, asking that the road in this catchment area be stopped.'

There was hesitation but finally it was agreed to, and two hundred women and children set out to walk to the next village. The logging licensee, also the provincial MP, was aware they were coming.

The day they went I was up in the bush again. A couple of days earlier, I'd walked with three boys and eight dogs up the headwaters of the Tawatana Stream.

I'd seen the licence and the loggers were not complying with their conditions. Trees were felled into the stream and branches left, while the licence stipulated that no trees be felled within twenty metres of the stream.

The dirt feeder roads were unsurfaced, when they were supposed to be surfaced. They were much wider than the five metres allowed and were already eroded.

As we climbed higher, I believed we were probably well over 400 metres, the height at which all logging was prohibited.

We passed damaged betelnuts and sago palms. The

sago palms had previously been used by villagers to build custom houses. As we crossed towards the dam, it began to rain. I sheltered under my umbrella with a ten-year-old boy. It was this rain that caused the first pollution of the water supply. The licensee later tried to claim it was a very heavy downpour.

'No,' I said. 'I was up there. It was just rain.'

Following an old path through four old villages on four separate ridges we came to a road Yankin Bayan were building that was on Billy's land. He had not given them permission to build the road. Coming down we passed the remnants of fruitless roadblocks Billy had built. Time after time, they were removed by landowners and loggers.

Down at the log point a number of felled Ngali Nuts logs were pointed out to me. This tree was specifically forbidden to be felled in the licence. A local non-government organisation had estimated that oil from a single ngali nut tree over its lifetime could fetch up to $SI20,000 or $A4000.

The day the women and children walked to see the licensee I was in the bush behind Ubuna where there was even more damage. My guides had seen a bulldozer washed into the stream, there was a feeder road within a couple of metres of the stream with dirt washing into the water.

Dirt on the bridge was also washing into the stream. Their licence stated all bridges were to be planked. Several times the road went through the stream.

The loggers finally had to leave this area. The

landowners successfully roadblocked the area when they began polluting the water supply. While we were in the bush we heard, but couldn't see, a RAMSI helicopter.

The last site we visited was a sacred site which had been bulldozed. There were three in this area. I later saw a document signed by the public solicitor calling for compensation. The bulldozer driver had been informed by a company employee of one of the sites but bulldozed it anyway.

On our way back, John, our guide, took us to a gorge where a stream entered a great cave. In the cool of the gorge, I was told of a snake with a light on its head and the bats and old skulls found in the caves. When Brian came back, John said, he was to bring a stout rope so they could explore them.

Back under the thatch of the hut we waited for John's grandmother to slowly come up from the village. She was in her eighties, a very wiry, bare-breasted woman, almost blind. Her name was Margaret.

While we waited, I drank a green coconut and admired the line of smoked pig jaws in the blackened rafters. Before Margaret shook my hand, she went to her small sleeping hut and put on a blouse in honour of our meeting. Then she told us the bad news. The licensee had refused to meet the Tawatana women and children.

When I got back, Tawatana was in an uproar. The young boys were on the road blocking all the company vehicles.

The next day at least there was peace on the roads. The licensee sent two retired policemen to negotiate. They returned to him with no solutions.

It became more and more difficult to get work done. I had paid a team to mill timber for my son's verandah. But they were an essential part of the roadblock team. The leader apologised.

'No, no,' I said. 'What you are doing is far more important.'

A strange signal was developed to call key people which made a noise like a ghostly police siren. On my last day there, it was impossible to hold a conversation. The whirring noise started time after time, and people disappeared. Billy had told me too, that the loggers had finally recognised I was a problem, and I was no longer to go anywhere on my own.

But it was too late.

The next day, May 5, I was leaving the village.

Chapter 12

THE WALK UP THE MAKIRA COAST AND HIV EDUCATION

It was a relief to finally leave the village. The tension had become unbearable.

I had complained about this the evening before and Billy's wife Audie said, 'And how much worse for those of us who live here.'

With guilty relief, I left. My two young male volunteers had not turned up by eight so I left alone. It was a pristine morning and even the log camp was peaceful, but people were curious.

'Where are you going?'

'To Wango, and then Kirakira.'

'What by leg?'

I nodded.

People smiled at me now. At first they were suspicious and had even mistaken me for the anthropologist's girlfriend. However, after seven meetings about HIV with Eunice in neighbouring villages, they knew me.

I decided to walk on the road rather than the beach. The

sea was enticing but the road was quicker. After a couple of hours, I arrived at Waimarae, the two-hundred-hectare coconut plantation that Eunice and her family owned.

As I waded through a swift flowing clean stream from the hills, I heard a logging ute behind me. Yankin Bayan had come to collect clean water. Having contaminated all the streams in their vicinity, they had to drive a considerable distance to get here, a luxury the local villagers didn't have.

When Eunice and I had walked to the coconut plantation, a couple of weeks earlier she told me the story. Her late husband Barnabas had bought the plantation from a Chinese man for $SI20,000 and they had spent many weekends here, Barnabas planting coconuts.

After his death, the land had been disputed, with the same provincial politician that was licensee for the logging company. He claimed it was his customary land and ownership of the land was initially granted to him. However there had been an appeal and the magistrate in Kirakira had determined it was no longer customary land and now belonged to Eunice and her family including a branch of the family who were Seventh Day Adventists (SDA).

An old man appointed by Barnabas was still living in an abandoned logging hut and more of his family were joining him. Meanwhile, villagers from the nearby village made gardens in the largely abandoned plantation. Roger, Brian's father-in-law, sent over some money to begin cleaning and developing it, but it was difficult to find people to work here. Some people still made easy money from logging, and

Chapter 12   The walk up the Makira Coast and HIV Education

it was two hours' hours walk from Tawatana.

I sat near a dilapidated copra shed and talked with Henry, one of the SDA relatives, about the tractor parts and new chainsaw he needed. The tractor, trailer and chainsaw had been working. He used them to mill timber and sold it to pay for his piece of land. A tyre had burst on the trailer and now it was blocking the road in solitary splendour, with vehicle marks around it.

On the other side of the plantation was the village of Asimanioha. I was resting in the whitewashed church, admiring the custom carvings and weaving when the boys arrived. They were breathless and laden with gear, including my large pack. I hoisted it on and we set off.

Andrew was a youth leader in Tawatana while Sam was a Save the Children's volunteer, the organisation that provided seventy per cent of condoms in the Solomons. Andrew and Sam had accompanied me during our seven education sessions on HIV, the first of which was held on the 22 April, the day after I arrived.

We had walked three hours to Marou Bay and three hours back. I was also accompanied by volunteers from the Mothers' Union of the Anglican Church. We ran a session at the primary school in Marou Bay with 50 children from 10-14 years and four teachers. Sam and I also spoke with the youth leader and left some condoms with him.

I was clear about the objective of the sessions. I wanted people to know that Papua New Guinea, fifteen years ago had six cases of HIV, the same number the

Solomons had now. In Papua New Guinea now there was a full-blown HIV/AIDs epidemic and many of the loggers now having sex with local girls had come from there. Vulnerable groups needed to understand how HIV/AIDS infected people, have access to condoms and be prepared to use them. As I had recently volunteered in a full-scale AIDS epidemic in Cambodia for eighteen months I had experience in this field.

While I was in Marou Bay I spoke with the clinic nurse. Many of the nurses remembered me as I had tutored them. During clinic visits I collected their sexually transmitted disease reports as agreed with the Nursing Director in Kirakira. We spoke about condom supply, family planning concerns, Pap smear screening and reports of women with cervical cancer.

It was midday but the boys said it was too early for lunch. They waited impatiently as further down the road I spoke to a short, stocky man in front of his large, corrugated-iron warehouse.

It had been a copra shed but people no longer made copra he said as there was no transport. Cacao was more profitable, but his rice mill was even more successful with people including students queuing up to mill their rice.

Finally, we arrived at Aringana, and sat on a bench under the shade of a big mango, drinking green coconuts. An older man with a beard arrived and introduced himself as a retired nursing officer I had worked with thirty years ago. He invited us to the clinic to speak with his wife. We talked about sexually transmitted disease and prevention. I gave her some of our most effective charts which she promised to use on clinic days. We had been warned not to stay at Aringana as many people supported logging. A logging ute stopped to let off a man who we recognised as the brother of an in-law who worked for Yankin Bayan.

'Sorry,' he said gleefully, 'There's no room for you on the ute.'

'That's okay, we enjoy walking,' I said.

It was almost dark when we walked through Yankin Bayan's base camp. The lights were on, and few people were about. An unregistered logging ute with no lights came towards us with no lights. They stopped and asked the boys what we were doing.

'Don't talk to them,' I said.

Well after six we arrived at Wango. Ten years before, I'd spent a night here on the nurse aide's veranda and been bitten mercilessly by fire-ants. The nurse aide had now left, and the post was deserted, but we were offered accommodation in a staff house the community had built.

I was very tired. I surveyed the dirty two-room hut in the dim light of the kerosene lamp with some dismay. Sarah, the registered nurse on leave in Wango, had suggested it.

As I watched a rat running into a pile of rubbish in one of the rooms I selfishly decided to take the other room.

I slept on my small Thermarest with a ground sheet sprayed with insecticide to keep the cockroaches off. My head was in a boxlike impregnated mosquito net which flowed over my bedsheet. My belongings were on the single table with a liberal spray of insecticide on the table legs. The boys slept all night with a kerosene lamp near the heap of rubbish and the rats were quiet.

In the predawn light I began making my preparations for my ablutions. Wango hadn't changed in the last ten years and there were still no toilets. Down at the beach there was flurry of men as I walked along the shore. I was obviously going the wrong way. I followed a woman around the long sandy bay, and finally secreted myself behind some bushes.

I made my way back through a bushy plantation, washed my hands in a small stream, avoided some human faeces on the road, and got back in time to see the boys emerging.

It was sunny and I decided to wash my clothes in a stream. The boys ate fried fish and boiled sweet potatoes while I found Weet-Bix and milk. The bell for our meeting rang, but I was worried about leaving our possessions unguarded. The boys talked first and then Andrew and I swapped for the condom demonstration.

When I got to the meeting, I found the people were weary, but they livened up when we divided the men and women and got on with the demonstration. The female condom provoked hilarity and even fear as the women gazed at the large plastic bag.

We set off for Macedonia, where Grace, Sam's mother, lived. Although tired. I enjoyed gazing at the islands of Ugi and Ulawa and Bio, home of the frigate birds. It was dusk when we arrived.

Macedonia was prettier than I remembered with leaf houses surrounding a large well-kept patch of clover. To one side was the church and Solomon Mamaloni's father's grave. Near the church was the prow of an orange fibreboard canoe jutting out from the ground. I shook hands with Mamaloni's mother-in-law, and his attractive, lively sisters.

It was almost dark when we got to Grace's school. We walked along the beach and entered a village where a woman was sweeping the ground. I looked at a long notice pinned to a pole. It said because of the recent number of elopements females wearing trousers, both long and short, were banned by the village committee. I panicked and told the boys they would have to ban me as I had nothing else to wear. Sam told me not to worry so we walked past the sign despite disapproving looks.

That evening, in the corrugated iron house lit by kerosene lamps, Grace, also known by Sam as Matron, fed me with ghost stories. She was a plump, cheerful woman with a similarly resolute female companion. She had been a schoolmistress for many years, and Sam and his sister had lived in many places. That explained why so many people knew him.

Sam was a ladies' man and had his own Matron and baby girl. Sam and family had not however paid the bride price for Matron junior, a rather timid looking girl. Young

Matron therefore could not accompany him back to Tawatana.

Grace's stories began after I saw a large flare dropping behind some trees. In the West, they would probably say it was some space junk, but here it unleashed a flood of stories about ghostly armies.

American soldiers with large packs had talked to villagers in local languages, noiseless boats had been seen, as had planes with flashing green and white lights. It was rumoured there was a huge underground army in a cave with an entrance near Marou Bay.

Grace said one European, currently living in the Tikopian settlement, had seen the cave and entrance but had been warned not to speak of it.

These sights began after the Second World War and Maasina Rule. Some people believed the Americans would return with abundant goods and distribute them. The sightings became more frequent after the death of Mamaloni, and following political unrest, including the recent burning of Chinatown.

Grace also told me about Mamaloni's death. He had been in Makira and was becoming increasingly ill but refused to go back to Honiara and fly to Australia as had been arranged. By the time he got to Honiara he was desperately ill, and Grace heard this news when she was in the bank. Mamaloni had asked for home-baked taro but when she brought it to him he was in the morgue. His wife Mary was clinging to his body and crying.

His funeral was held on the other side of Makira, and I'd already heard stories about the strange Europeans who had turned up whom no-one else knew. Grace knew one European couple and had been charged by Mamaloni to look after them.

The next morning after prising Sam from his Matron and baby we were back on the road about eleven. It was gently raining. As we neared the largest river, we left the road and made our way to a ford closer to the coast. We crossed with the water up to our chests and held our belongings above our heads. At the usual road crossing, Sam said we would have been swimming.

Before we came to the crossing, we walked through Nuku, a settlement straggling alongside the road for many kilometres and inhabited by Tikopians.

Solomon Mamaloni arranged for them to come many years ago as their island had become too small for their growing population.

At the nurse aide post, the nurse said he had worked alone for ten years. He had no condoms but had won an award for being very active with family planning. The Tikopians had limited land and were concerned about large families. We gave him some condoms and Sam and Andrew promised to hold an HIV/AIDS awareness meeting with him on their return trip.

A logging ute went past with the name Middle Island emblazoned on it. Sam told me the company had a good reputation, kept their licence conditions and assisted with community development. We walked past the new school AUSAID had built. NZAID also supported villages with building more classrooms in Makira but had a more inclusive approach. Villages around Makira were building the classrooms with materials NZAID donated. Their development consultant in Kirakira also supported the professional development of teachers.

Our host that evening was Hilda, George's niece, and her husband. After leaving our gear, we walked to Pamua, a large Anglican secondary school and arranged with the headmaster to talk to five-hundred students in the morning. We were up at dawn as the appointment was for soon after seven. After waiting half an hour, we were sent to the church. Slowly students began to filter in and when they were all present, they began singing, led by the deputy head boy. One-and-a-half hours later they were still singing and there were no staff except Father Abel.

He went to the staff room, came back with the news the teachers were meeting and told me to go and see them. I did and was told I could begin speaking to the students.

The teachers came over to listen and afterwards the students were given a day off. I heard later there were management problems in the school.

Waimapuru, the government school we spoke at that evening, was well organised. The students were interested and the questions went on for one-and-a-half hours. Finally, I said I would stay behind and answer private questions because it was getting late. Some of the questions were extraordinary. I assured one teenage boy who asked about the risk of having sex with a corpse who had died of AIDS that he would not be attracted to an AIDS victim.

'You would be sleeping with a skeleton,' I said.

In the early morning I went down to see the nurse aide who was on her way to Honiara and had shut the clinic at Kaonasugu. She said she was still becoming familiar with the clinic as she had just been there a month, so I entertained myself watching her small relative with a knife.

He was eighteen months old and they said he played with knives all the time. He had a long kitchen knife and was expertly mimicking cutting a nut. Then he made a few chops at the log he was sitting on and began quartering a smaller stick, imitating an adult chopping up tobacco. Very impressed, I wondered aloud if he had ever cut himself.

They didn't seem sure but replied, 'Not recently.'

That morning, as we were beginning our last three-hour walk to Kirakira, we chanced upon the bishop's transport and gratefully accepted a lift.

The landscape changed. The coconut plantations were brushed, the grass underneath cut short and looked operational. Sometimes cacao bushes provided an understorey. There were more and flasher permanent buildings.

I had been flying in and out of Kirakira for thirty years and it had changed. The only transport used to be Jack Campbell's tractor but now there were logging company utes, the medical truck, the church truck, the bishop's vehicle, two RAMSI vehicles and boat, and even a taxi.

There was a bakery, but the bread sold out by 6 am. There were numerous rest houses catering for Asian loggers, AUSAID, European Union and World Bank officials, Greenpeace employees and miscellaneous people like me. There was also a market which sold betelnut, leaf to chew with it, green coconuts and little else.

It's a relaxed place. A stranger stands out quickly, but then after thirty years I'm not a stranger. The first people to approach me were the nurses, many of whom I had worked with. There was no doctor. Later I learnt they had had a very good one but he had fallen out with the Premier over the standard of housing for hospital staff. We discussed various patients including the short woman with probable cephalon-pelvic disproportion with her first baby. They medicated her to stop labour and planned to evacuate her to Honiara. There was the eight-year-old with possible meningitis, positive malaria and severe fitting which they managed to control.

I saw the nursing director in Kirakira and gave him the report about the clinics. I also met the Save the Children Fund coordinator, thanked him for Sam's help, and told him about our program including condom distribution.

I was also worried about the logging. First, I went to see the Makira Conservation Fund (MCF), the organisation Billy had met with. Here I met Canadian volunteer Mat and Victor, the Solomon Islands director. The situation seemed overwhelming with some of the logging operations sounding even worse than Yankin Bayan.

Under the forestry legislation, there were two means of suspending logging if licence conditions weren't complied with. The public solicitor in Honiara had the powers to suspend logging but rarely visited. Forestry officials also had these powers but the officer in Kirakira was completely uninterested. I gave Mat and Victor details of all the licence breaches I had observed and was invited to meet some visiting European Union (EU) officials that evening.

Back at John Wesley and Alison's house I heard news about Tawatana. The situation was alarming. The police had been down from Kirakira and wanted to arrest people including Billy. However, the villagers had said these people were acting on their behalf and if they wanted to arrest anyone they would have to arrest the whole village.

John Wesley, Alison, and I discussed the presentation we would make to the EU officials. Alison, Eunice's daughter, was a primary school teacher, John a senior administrator with the Church of Melanesia. The meeting that evening was a watershed. The EU officials were interested, even concerned, and suggested various approaches. The business development officer for the province, who was touring with the party, also expressed concern.

On my return that evening to the Anglican church rest house where I was staying, I found twenty priests had arrived. The bishop had called them all for a meeting. I spoke to Father Godfrey from Tawatana. He had spent the previous day trying to persuade the youths of the village not to burn down the loggers' camp. The blockade had finished with the verbal assurance from the company they would stop building the road affecting the water supply. Yankin Bayan had broken this verbal agreement and were still constructing the road.

In the morning, I went to see RAMSI, represented by a pleasant young Australian policeman. I took him a copy of the licence breaches and explained the background. He was sympathetic but did not believe forestry issues were a police responsibility.

John Wesley now had a plan. We learnt that the company did not have a current business licence with the province and was therefore operating illegally. John took the letter outlining the licence breaches to the provincial secretary and got him to admit the company no longer had a business licence and therefore was illegal. John wrote the minutes of this meeting and got the provincial secretary to sign these.

He also drafted a petition to be sent back with the priest for the villagers to sign in Tawatana, urging that Makira province did not issue a business licence. John Wesley said he would then go down by canoe to Tawatana, hold a meeting and collect the petition.

Although the plane was scheduled it didn't turn up for two days and accommodation was becoming a problem. I had left the church rest house to the priests and gone to the most expensive rest house which had a washing machine. I then had to move out again to make way for the return of the EU officials. The nurses came to my rescue and I spent my last night peacefully in a two-bedroom house.

On Saturday, I met the Malaysian Yankin Bayan loggers at the airport and later heard the story. They had trespassed on land they had no right to be on and had been chased away with machetes. The man who leased bulldozers to them had taken fright at all the opposition and reclaimed his bulldozers.

On Saturday, however, none of us left Kirakira, including the pregnant woman with the suspected cephalon-pelvic disproportion. The plane flew overhead full of passengers from the Reef Islands.

On Monday, when we finally boarded the plane, the Malaysians took the single seats with the best view and were able to see better than I the roads, the destruction, they had wrought on the island.

It wasn't until I left the Solomons that I understood that during the RAMSI intervention logging, rather than declining, had tripled in volume between 2002 and 2004. At the same time, the logging royalties collected by the government had dropped by $SI30 million. This evidence was presented in two Solomon Islands Government reports, the Ministry of Natural Resources, 2005, and the Office of the Auditor General, 2005. Both documents were accessed from website www.masalai-i-tokout.com, (2006).[234] This website has been described by the Papua New Guinea Forestry Department as a source which from June 2002 has published more than fifty short reports based on leaked documents from within the Papua New Guinea Forest Authority and other government departments.

I have copies of my letters to the Commissioner of Forests, Solomon Islands, to the editor of the *Australian*, and to the *Solomons Star*. No one was interested except for a New Zealand friend, Tony Johns. He was a lawyer and retired permanent secretary from New Zealand who continued to do consultancy work in the Pacific. He said I was lucky not to be permanently banned from the Solomons.

When I arrived back in Honiara, I had twenty-four hours to finish my business. Honiara was dusty, dirty, hot, and this time burnt out. I looked at the shell of the casino. The frames of burnt-out cars still stood in front of it. I heard stories later in Australia of customers chased up the stairs by an angry mob and finally rescued by RAMSI. The destruction seemed very selective. A few buildings were still standing with charred remains on either side.

I heard later these shops belonged to long term Chinese residents who had paid for protection. Reconstruction work had already started on some of the hyphen less damaged properties.

I had only one evening in Honiara so George came up to Alice and Kendrick's house where I was staying. George was as busy as ever, but this time as a policy analyst for the Opposition.

I went to see the AUSAID project officer at the Ministry of Health. She seemed surprised by the work I had done and said the report was good. We agreed I should send her my master's thesis on cervical cancer in the Solomons, although it was six years out of date. During this visit to Makira, I found that in every village women knew of others who had died.

We discussed the possibility of a pilot program for cervical cancer vaccine. She felt WHO might support it. I also met the coordinator of the national HIV/AIDS program and the education director of the Solomon Islands Planned Parenthood Association. We spoke of the problems around the family planning program in Makira and the misconceptions some people had.

Finally at the airport, with leisure to reflect, I thought of my past visit and my hopes for the future. Perhaps next time I would have a chance to swim, to dive, to explore caves. But although it had been a hard visit and a difficult one, it had been worthwhile. One of the most special moments had been on my second to last day at Tawatana, just before Billy told me I was not to go anywhere alone.

I was sitting on the ancient coastal rock Billy felt was so special, jutting into the sea. Beside me in the rock were very old engravings of frigate birds and fish. This area had been one of Rebi's favorite haunts.

This was near the area that had been preserved by the family elders when they refused to allow it to become a logging point; the area that so many people now came to on the weekends to picnic, swim and relax.

I was sitting quietly watching the waves breaking on the reef when I distinctly heard the words, 'Thank You.'

'No trouble. I'm happy to be here,' I thought looking out to sea.

Chapter 13

INTRODUCTION OF CERVICAL CANCER VACCINE AND ISABEL

In 2006, when Professor Ian Frazer and the late Dr Jian Zhou announced the discovery of a vaccine against the Human Papilloma Virus (HPV), the virus that causes cervical cancer I, along with millions of others, was delighted. In 2007, Australia became the first country in the world to roll out the Gardasil vaccine.[235]

In 2007, the Australian Cervical Cancer Foundation (ACCF) was formed, its goal to eliminate cervical cancer in the developing world. Joe Tooma was the chief executive officer and Professor Frazer the scientific adviser.

A pathologist and colleague of my father, Dr John Mayze, introduced me to Dr Roger Maraka, the first Solomon Islands pathologist when he visited Brisbane in November 2008. Dr Mayze suggested we approach Joe at the ACCF. We did this and attended a meeting with Dr Margaret McAdams, a GP who was working with the ACCF in Vanuatu. Dr McAdams suggested the Solomons consider applying for a pilot vaccine program through the Global Alliance Vaccine Initiative (GAVI).

In March 2009, when Dr Maraka was again in Australia, we met Joe and the executive of ACCF. A proposal was then sent to the Solomon Islands Ministry of Health proposing that ACCF and the Ministry work together on an application to GAVI. This proposal was accepted and in June 2013 Joe, myself and my son Brian, an IT project manager, flew to the Solomons to provide support. It was a daunting task. There was a twenty-three-page application document and guidelines of the same length.

The goal was to plan for a two-year pilot vaccine program for up to 10,000 girls in two locations, develop a national cervical cancer strategy and an adolescent health intervention program.

Many stakeholders needed to be involved including WHO, UNICEF, Ministry of Women's Affairs, Health Education, the Council and Provincial officials concerned and Non-Government Organisations such as churchwomen's groups. GAVI advised an Inter-Agency Coordinating Group be set up to steer the process and liaise with the International Consultant Doctor Scott LaMontagne from PATH. Feeding into this were four working groups including the Vaccine Delivery Working Group.

That first evening, our first goal was achieved. We attended a Rotary meeting and one of the Rotarians agreed to provide me with accommodation for the first three months.

There were whirlwind visits with Joe during the three days he was with us. Before he left, he had signed a renewed memorandum of understanding with the Permanent Secretary, Dr Ross, which included the appointment of a local program coordinator.

Brian stayed two weeks and assisted me with the terms of reference for both the Inter-Agency Coordinating Group and working groups and was there for the inaugural meetings.

While Brian was there, we went to see George and Martha Ngeingari. George Atkin was now living with them. It was a sad story. George had been on the street for two years when George and Martha found him outside the Central Bank of the Solomon Islands one night. He was sick and exhausted, and they took him home. They had gone out to buy baby formula for their granddaughter who they adopted after their daughter died in childbirth.

Eventually he got another job and I often met up with him. At one point we met the Taiwanese ambassador together who urged me to visit a Taiwanese ship paying a friendly visit to the Solomons. I declined. I felt it important to remain politically neutral. When George and I were together, he sometimes pointed out places where he had slept. He also maintained that desperate midnight prayers went straight to God. Meanwhile I was living in a big house with a harbour view in a self-contained flat downstairs. It was an easy walk to the hospital.

My first job was to recruit a local coordinator and

this I did with the help of the local nurses. We recruited Veerah who had trained at the SDA Hospital in Malaita. Veerah found a room to rent, not easy in Honiara, and Joe supported her with an accommodation budget.

We also had to quickly identify another pilot area for the vaccine aside from Honiara. We considered the Guadalcanal Plains, just south of Honiara, spoke to provincial officials and carried out a reconnaissance tour. There weren't enough girls. Then I thought of Isabel and went to see Rosalie.

She thought Isabel would be delighted to take part and advised me to ring her daughter Sarah who was the doctor and acting director of health in Isabel. Sarah said she was interested so Veerah and I booked our passage to Buala, the provincial capital.

We arrived in Buala at 2 am. Although we had booked rooms at the Mothers' Union rest house, it was in darkness. We had nowhere else to sleep so we banged on the door and woke a resident. They let us in and we slept on chairs in the dining area until the morning when a rather apologetic woman gave us rooms.

First we went to see Jimmy Habu, the Premier. He was reserved, but said if the Health, Nursing and Education directors agreed, it was all right with him.

First, we met with Dr Sarah Dyer. We were welcomed and introduced to the hospital staff at the early morning meeting, including the deputy director of nursing and some of the nurse managers from the district health clinics.

If I had any doubts about Isabel, the deputy director of nursing, Helen M, overturned them. She begged us to come. She was so saddened by the women who kept presenting with cervical cancer in a palliative stage. They were sent to Honiara, the diagnosis confirmed, and then sent back to die in their villages. Beside taking part in the pilot vaccine program, she wanted PAP smears to be available to women in Buala.

Patricia, the reproductive health nurse, was keen to be trained to take PAP smears. We arranged for her to stay in Honiara and do an attachment with Solomon Islands Planned Parenthood Association (SIPPA). Their nurses were trained by a nurse from the New South Wales Family Planning Association.

Everyone was keen. Andy, the nurse in charge of distributing vaccines, was hardworking and capable. The province had a high uptake of child immunisations, a GAVI requirement. We spoke with the Director of Education and then an official who provided the numbers of nine- to twelve-year-old female students. Unlike Honiara, there seemed few girls who were not at school.

I knew from Rosalie that Isabel was run by a troika, the Government, the Anglican church and the Council of Chiefs. We walked around the point to meet the Vicar General, Father Ausley. Besides the church, there was residential accommodation for those from rural areas who had come to do courses. We also met the archbishop's wife, Moira, who was also a member of the Council of

Chiefs. She introduced me to half a dozen chiefs, and they became a critical part of our sensitisation and mobilisation campaign in Isabel.

Many of the chiefs were married to retired nurses and we trained them too. Because of the cohesion of the society and the enthusiasm of all involved, I went back to Honiara from Isabel confident the plan and program would work.

Back in Honiara, Brian told me over the phone that he had a half-sister and a half-brother. I wasn't surprised as George and I had been divorced for decades. I wondered why George hadn't told me. Rebecca was sixteen and lived with her mother in a village in Bauro, closer to Kirakira. We had coffee together. Sadly she missed a lot of school because of constant bouts of malaria. She was very proud to be an Atkin and very keen to meet Brian and John. When she went back to Makira, I gave her money to buy a bike to get to school.

Harry was a couple of years younger. His mother was from Isabel and she and George had lived together for a while. I gave Harry a few books. Later, he went through a difficult patch, but I understand he is now back in Isabel and doing okay. Brian remains in touch with Rebecca and has supported her to visit Australia and encouraged her to become both a businesswoman and a cacao farmer.

The consultant, Dr Scott LaMontagne, arrived. The most important planning, including the budget, had been completed. It had been difficult to find qualified people to undertake research and evaluation and Scott said he

Chapter 13 Introduction of Cervical Cancer Vaccine and Isabel

would supervise this. Brian flew over and helped finalise the application and it was submitted.

On 20 May 2014 we heard the application was one of eight worldwide GAVI approved. GAVI offered to support a two-year HPV vaccination program from April 2015. They would provide two doses of Gardasil vaccine for up to 8000 schoolgirls. The girls would be aged from nine to twelve in the first year and in the second year nine-year-olds would be offered the vaccine.

Joe Tooma, Brian and I flew to the Solomons in June 2014 and met Dr La Montagne, Veerah and other stakeholders to begin planning.

On 11 June, the Inter-Agency Coordinating Committee (ICC) meeting concluded that only two doses of the vaccine were needed six months apart. Previously it had been three.

Logistics of the operation including the procurement, the storage space, the cold chain and the communication strategy were discussed at the Technical Assistance Group meeting, held in the afternoon. The availability of canoes in Isabel was also discussed and I was advised I could stay at Jubilee House in the hospital compound, with overseas medical students doing a placement.

The following is a description of my stay in Jubilee House, written in my diary towards the end of 2014:

> With great reluctance, I wheeled my suitcases down to the spacious lobby in the Mendana Hotel. It was impossible to stay for ten weeks there at $SBD1000 a night (A$250),

because unlike the well paid DFAT advisers funded by Australian taxpayers, ACCF would not foot such a bill.

Heading from the Mendana to the hospital the taxi got stuck in traffic. In thirty-five years, the road and bridges haven't changed despite the burgeoning population and number of vehicles. It would have been quicker to walk, but not with three suitcases. George was with me. I'm not sure what I expected him to do if there wasn't any room at Jubilee House. All the relatives' houses were overflowing.

It was late afternoon when we arrived, and the house was open. Two slightly flustered young women, who I learnt later were English medical students, looked at me and my three suitcases with trepidation.

'Is he staying, too?' they asked of George.

We all looked at him. George's spectacles had lost an arm on one side which gave him a lopsided look. Unlike his two sons, he wasn't losing his hair, instead it sprang in wild grey corkscrews from his head. He was wearing ladies' pants donated by me hitched up by a belt, and a secondhand shirt with a grubby collar. He had thongs on his feet.

'No,' I said hastily.

'We have just cleaned your room,' the two women said together, introducing themselves as K and K.

'That's very sweet,' I said trying to fit the three suitcases into the small room with two beds.

Chapter 13 Introduction of Cervical Cancer Vaccine and Isabel

'Well, I am here for three months,' I said by way of excuse.

Short K and tall K went out later and I sat in the dark when the lights went out.

'Sorry we didn't show you,' they said hastily on their return.

'It's solar as well as prepaid and when the water stops you go outside and turn the pump on.'

The ceiling fans were grimy with the black oil from the diesel fumes from the traffic outside. There were a lot of bush mechanics in the town and a lot of poorly maintained cars. As time went by, I wondered if the constriction I could feel in my airways and the occasional wheeze, was my imagination or the effects of air pollution.

At midnight the fans went off. I woke in a lather and as instructed, turned the power back on at the mains. Later that day, a small boy dropped a docket on the kitchen table. That night when the water had stopped, and I went out to turn on the pump I saw the electric cord which stretched over to the next house. When I spoke of this, the girls shrugged. We managed to get it unhooked, but our relations with the neighbours deteriorated as they had been getting free power for their barbecue.

We lived among the houses for lab technicians and nurses. Further down were the houses of the domestics. Many families, to supplement their income ran a barbecue. For hungry medical students coming back from the wards too tired to cook, this was a welcome alternative although many of the chickens weren't cooked until 8 pm.

I became more selective about the places I frequented after twice witnessing the delivery of chickens to the barbecue next door. I saw them arrive through the slats of the fence. I had never seen such miserable hens. Although many were still alive, some were already dead. There were many bald red places where their feathers had been rubbed away, and they were suspiciously large, six-week chickens raised on hormones. Now I understood the questions village men had anxiously asked me about whether eating chicken would 'unman' them. I realised there was a good chance of it.

The lady butchered the live ones and dismembered all of them, throwing their legs to the scrawny dogs. No nonsense about food hygiene regulations here and none about cruelty to animals either. There was an ever-growing pile of beer cans in her yard. From time to time, she would get drunk and there would be loud music all night. When I was really exasperated, I would take my Thermarest and light sleeping bag and bunk down in the kitchen which was just a little further away.

There were other little shops run behind people's houses. The two Ks would often disappear after getting back from the hospital for their shot of pineapple Fanta, impossible to buy in either England, or Australia. Nearer the hospital was a stall where women sold cooked eggs, fish and chips, slices of melon, cooked taro, and cooked bananas, all remarkably healthy. The only thing I declined was the fish as they came from the harbour, where the sewer went.

We were a hundred metres from the sea and we could hear the waves. I enjoyed walking to the sea and watching the sunsets, however, I mused it wasn't an ideal position for a hospital in view of tsunamis and rising sea levels. There were plans to resite it.

Slowly, the two Ks and I got to know each other. They would debrief with me when they got home. The older taller K was finding it difficult to sleep. There was a lot of night life with sex workers, touts, drunks laughing and shouting outside. Taxis with huge amplifiers would stop for barbecues. The bass was so loud the boom would reverberate right through the house.

The older K would wake exhausted, and get to the wards a little later, while young K in her early twenties and bristling with energy had adopted the children's ward and they had adopted her. She took notes and helped put IVs in babies. She said it was taxing for a third-year medical student, especially with the type of needles they had.[236]

From other staff, I heard about the child who died because there was no oxygen over the weekend, the women who couldn't be tested for urinary protein because there were no urine tests, the operations that couldn't be carried out because there was no sterile linen, the woman with the cardiac symptoms who couldn't have an ECG because there was no tracing paper. Ward clerks were needed and a good hospital administrator.

Finding patients' charts was another problem. The chart room was a small room with labelled boxes from which charts often never emerged. There was general rejoicing when the consultant who had admitted someone a few weeks previously managed to find their earlier chart.

I heard the labour ward was challenging, especially in October nine months after the previous Christmas. The labour beds had no mattresses so the metal base could be easily disinfected between deliveries. Women were sometimes given medication to speed up labour, while husbands weren't allowed. A two-tiered system had emerged with private obstetricians.

I began to socialise more, mixing with the health staff from Aspen the private hospital solely for RAMSI staff who were healthy. The staff sat there waiting for emergencies, while the Australian taxpayer paid. Meanwhile, the hospital lab had lost 80 per cent of its funding and there was some doubt whether the Solomon Islands School of Nursing would continue.

During this time ten newly trained Cuban doctors arrived. They had been sent to Cuba to train and knew Spanish but had no practical experience with patients. Kiribati trained them for six months and then supervised them for two years. The Solomons came to a similar arrangement.

Dr Scott LaMontagne arrived in August 2014 during a measles epidemic and a number of deaths. Numerous banners urged people to get vaccinated, a measles ward had been set up, health education officers used loud hailers at the markets and vaccination tents were set up.

Dr LaMontagne was there a week and the vaccine order was resubmitted and the plan confirmed. Honiara and Isabel were to hold a workshop with senior nurses and other stakeholders and submit their budgets.

When the consultant left, not surprisingly it was impossible to meet with anyone, but Veerah and I managed to contact the key stakeholders to organise the budget workshops for both provinces. We also, after consulting stakeholders, began drafting some educational material which was reviewed by key ministry officials. We also began, with the health promotion team, to visit schools.

We had a few weeks to get around to forty schools and when the health promotion team indicated they would not always be available I thought of the retired nurses. This is serendipity I thought, when I met one of the retired nurses outside the Ministry of Health building. She was happy to help and so were six of her colleagues, so I trained them. I booked a hospital car, arranged a daily payment, and we were off. It was good to be working with them again. I told a younger colleague about it, and rather rudely she said she hoped no-one would die on the job. They were a great help.

Veerah and I visited the eight Honiara clinics and spoke with the nurses and clinic supervisors. I also contacted the Soroptimists who funded two provincial training workshops and the initial educational material. There was a GAVI budget, but there were such stringent safeguards it was often difficult to access.

After the completion of the measles campaign there was a week before the trachoma campaign started and we held the Honiara budget workshop then.

We kept in touch with Isabel and Veerah toured with the Isabel nurses when they toured for the measles campaign and spoke with the clinic nurses.

At the same time, Amanda arrived, an experienced midwife and family planner who Joe had recruited for four weeks. I was delighted to see her and so were the doctors. She was promptly invited to provide counselling to women in their twenties, thirties and forties who were dying of cervical cancer.

Amanda also worked with the clinic nurses and identified that although their technique was good, they were using the wrong kind of brush and not enough fixative. I spoke with the laboratory manager and found the fixative was running low and had not been reordered. He rectified this.

A couple of weeks after Amanda arrived, early in November 2014, we flew over to Isabel to take part with the EPI manager and UNICEF representative to conduct the planning workshop.

When we walked out to the plane, I was glad to see it was not a six-seater. A week earlier Veerah had flown back in a six-seater and was alarmed when she saw drops of fuel on the engine. She nudged the person in front, who nudged the next person and finally the pilot became aware of it. He told them to put their emergency jackets on and flew the plane on the other engine. The pilot radioed ahead to Honiara, where they landed with the fire truck and ambulance at the ready. There was a photo of Veerah pale and terrified in her bright orange jacket on the front page of the paper the next day.

This one-hour flight was more sedate. When we landed the oncoming passengers crowded around the plane.

We found our bags but later realised we had left our food behind, and we were convinced it had either been flown back to Honiara or been stolen.

Andy was waiting for us with the hospital canoe. It was a difficult time for him. His wife had just flown over to Honiara as her father was in hospital. There was another course going at the same time as ours, but I knew about it and had spoken with the coordinator.

I had forgotten how clean Isabel was, and how beautiful. We sniffed the clean air. It was such a break from the diesel fumes of Honiara. We walked through the bushes on to the sand beach and got into the canoe. As we surged past the other canoes, I looked up at the hills, the blue sky, and at the little town we were heading for.

'At last, the true Solomons,' I said to Amanda. 'It's not fair if you only see Honiara.'

Transport in Isabel is by canoe and the airport is an island. The roads don't penetrate far although the forty logging companies in residence built roads to get timber down to the logging points and waiting barges. Once the logging companies have left termites eat away the wooden bridges and the roads are washed away.

During our time we saw canoes laden with sand for building projects, people carrying market and that day we passed a boy, about six, in a small dugout with a stick for a paddle, playing in the shallows. Andy pulled up near him in front of the Mothers' Union Rest House.

We waded in and vainly we looked for the woman in charge. However, there was a European election volunteer staying and she rang for us. A harassed sounding woman said she had just got home but would be back shortly. We had booked during the week.

We finally got into our rooms, then went shopping and bought noodles, tinned fish, tinned tomatoes and rice.

We found the Mothers' Union rest house homely, with its large airy louvred lounge, embroidered plant hangings, cane chairs and tributes on the wall to the founder.

Going to work in the morning we passed men digging the trenches then preparing the foundations of a house. It was on a hill, the ground looked stony and they were toiling with picks and shovels. At lunch we passed them again, and at 4 pm they were still working. The foundations were deeper, and they had started to lay concrete. I waved at them. I couldn't help myself. The work ethic here is so impressive. Many times in Honiara I had passed labourers high on the scaffolding of numerous Chinese buildings, dreamily holding a hammer.

In the morning as we passed the airline's office, we were called in. They had our food bag. We confirmed our flight back in three days.

The next three days were hectic. We had a day to meet the hospital staff and everyone else and hold the two-day workshop. There was another five-day workshop elsewhere, which the clinic managers were attending. I had got wind of it in Honiara and had spoken with the facilitator and arranged to 'borrow' them for one day.

In the evening, we swapped stories with the Australians here to support the election officials. In Isabel everything was under control. There were ten people in a tiny office, but it worked. I said it was the same for us. This was a province that got things done.

The workshop went well. On the first day, we met the chiefs who wanted to help with their wives and a budget was made. On the second day the clinic managers, with some input from Amanda, put together a budget.

That afternoon we were whisked away by the airline's agent back to the airfield. It was such an idyllic place, on the beach in the shade waiting for the plane. There was a young woman newly delivered exhausted and jaundiced, being flown to the hospital. Andy had another family crisis. One of his wife's relatives had been killed when a tree fell on him during a logging operation. His body was being taken back to his village and his mother at that point hadn't been told of her son's death.

Just before we boarded the plane, one of the health

promotion officers rushed up. He gave me a big hug and thanked us for the workshop. It had been difficult to fit it in with the measles epidemic, the trachoma program and the other workshop, but we had managed.

I've never been hugged by a strange Solomon Islands man before and I told Amanda later I didn't think it was culturally appropriate.

'Perhaps they're just very grateful,' she said.[237]

Chapter 14

HONIARA PREPARATION, VACCINE LAUNCH, SCREENING AND TREATMENT

Back in Honiara as the national election grew closer, young men in army camouflage appeared on the streets. There was a big exodus as people returned to their provinces and villages to vote. George's restrictions grew tighter and I was no longer allowed to walk up the hill past the Anglican cathedral. K and K had left, and although I missed them it was easier. They were so leggy and attractive they attracted a cacophony of wolf whistles when we were out.

I moved out of Jubilee House before I left to go back to Australia for medical treatment over the Christmas break. I was persuaded by midwife H (European but raised in the Solomons) to share her rented unit. I inspected it and it seemed fine but it was very different at night. It was opposite the Pacific Casino and, as George informed me, in the middle of a cesspit of kwaso (illegal alcohol) brewers. The first night I was there someone tried to get through the window and I saw the shadow of his hand. H's brother put up security lights. Every night a nearby band practiced very loudly and very late. One night I heard a woman screaming for help and called the police. While I was in Australia, I had earplugs custom-made at a gunsmith's shop.

George went to hospital for an operation to remove a corneal growth. He had vision problems from diabetic retinopathy in his other eye and was completely blind after his surgery. I took turns with other relatives looking after him. Martha cooked and we took food to him. I enjoyed being with him in the hospital getting to know the other patients and their families. We all enjoyed the visits of the gentle and kind Anglican sisters. The most unpleasant task was guiding George through the flooded toilet block to the smelly pedestal.

One of the students staying with George and Martha was pale and I took him to a private GP. He was diagnosed with rheumatic heart disease, admitted to hospital, and commenced monthly penicillin injections which may be lifelong. In Australia, this disease is also common in Aboriginal communities, where there is overcrowding and a high bacterial load.

I visited our one-time neighbours and friends in Vura, Betty and Francis. Betty was in bed in the sitting room completely paralysed after a stroke, while Francis was in a wheelchair. Their daughters, Jacinta and Christina, cared for them with other relatives. They learnt their house was riddled with termites while I was there. The builder, who was a relative, had taken the hardwood Francis milled for the house and used untreated timber.

Dr La Montagne flew in before I left to discuss the Honiara and Isabel project budgets. He was happy with them but worked on the evaluation budget. He also saw the RAMSI accountant who assured him the GAVI budget would be available for the implementation of the vaccine program.

Finally, I could turn my attention to the screening of older women. The development of a cervical cancer strategy was part of this project and one of the working groups had been researching it. We had been in touch with Professor Glen Mola, an experienced obstetrician and gynaecologist who worked in Papua New Guinea. He advised the most appropriate strategy was visual inspection with acetic acid or VIA. Cellular changes were detected immediately and the woman could be treated on the spot or referred if necessary.

The working group delegated me to get in touch with the NSW Family Planning Association, the same organisation which supported Fiji with a VIA program.

One of their trainers already visited the Solomon Islands Planned Parenthood Association and provided PAP smear training programs. Following discussion, their senior executives agreed to a preliminary visit in 2015 to assess the possibility of setting up a pilot VIA program in the Solomons.

I came back in February 2015. All went well with the launch in late April and the vaccination program in both Honiara and Isabel. In Honiara, the pilot program reached seventy-two per cent of the girls in the target group, while in Isabel it was ninety-one per cent.[238]

In mid-April 2015, we had a high-level meeting about the coming NSW Family Planning visit with the WHO representative, the obstetrician/gynaecologist and the acting reproductive health coordinator. We wanted to identify the possible numbers of women requiring surgery after the screening program to ensure the Ministry of Health could meet this demand.

I had discussed the meeting with Joe previously and he suggested we use the figures from ACCF's experience in Nepal. The VIA program there found when two thousand women were screened around one hundred and twenty required surgery. There were around two thousand women in the target population in Honiara, the Guadalcanal Plains and Isabel. These areas were chosen because as a result of the vaccination program people there were already more educated about cervical cancer.

The team agreed there would be capacity to provide surgery to women who needed it. They also decided the program should include the identification and treatment of sexually transmitted diseases, including referral to the nearby clinic for partner tracing.

Fungal infections were to be treated and women with other gynaecological problems such as prolapse referred.

The possibility of obtaining visiting obstetricians and gynaecologists from a Pacific scheme was also discussed.

The visit of the NSW FPA executives was a success and they agreed to partner with the Solomon Islands Government to commence a VIA program with the three sites selected. Meanwhile, the PAP smear program was to continue.

I was almost ready to leave when a man I had been talking with one day dropped dead the next. He was in his early sixties and had high blood pressure.

Over the years, I have watched the health of Solomon Islanders, particularly in Honiara, deteriorate. Fruit and vegetables were more expensive. Before, people made gardens in the hills, but now that land was covered in houses. Chinese shops were everywhere, selling noodles, white bread, rice, sugar and alcohol. The ground was littered with plastic from ice block sticks. Finding something healthy to buy for lunch was difficult. The fishing village now sold small, very salty fish, the bycatch of the trawlers. This poor diet led to an epidemic of diabetes. In 2021, the Solomons had the sixth highest rate of diabetes in the world at twenty per cent. The highest was Tahiti at twenty-five per cent. In Australia the rate is between six and seven per cent.[239] We have relatives who have died of diabetes as have many other Solomon Islands families.

I also noticed that after the 'Tension' people's attitudes changed. Life was so hard they were focused on survival and there was less trust than before. Nurses with their family responsibilities worked hard at work and hard at home and were often exhausted. There were more people wandering around the street homeless, more people who looked drug affected, drunk or simply mentally unstable. There was hatred in some people's eyes.

I didn't get back to Makira while I was working on the project, and I was sorry. I met some Tawatana men in Honiara and they asked me why I hadn't been back and I said I was too busy. At least the vaccine program has now reached Makira.

The HPV national vaccination program was launched in the Solomons in May 2019 with 40,000 girls vaccinated initially and 8,000 annually after that.[240] It is likely that as in Bhutan, which began using HPV in 2010, that the risk of vaccinated girls dying from cervical cancer will be reduced by eighty per cent.[241]

NSW Family Planning began a pilot screening and treatment project between 2015 and 2018 in Honiara, the Guadalcanal Plains and Isabel. Following a review, the Solomon Islands Ministry of Health and key stakeholders agreed it be extended to the Western and Malaita Provinces in 2019 and 2020. Before 2020, eighty-nine clinicians were trained and 9000 women screened.

NSW Family Planning is now working on a national cervical cancer screening and treatment program and aims to have every woman of reproductive age screened within the next three to five years.[242] It has also introduced thermal ablation devices for treatment, which are more portable, battery-operated and been recommended by WHO since September 2019.²⁴³

Although COVID-19 has interrupted the ability to travel in the past two years, thermal ablation devices have been sent to the Solomon Islands in 2020 with the support of the Department of Foreign Affairs and Trade. It has also provided remote support to the program which in 2020 screened 2,500 women.

Dr Jagilly, the hospital superintendent, was very keen to upgrade the cancer treatment program by improving facilities at the hospital and seeking support from cancer specialists and he achieved this.

In September 2018, a specialist medical oncology team from Canberra, including medical oncologist Professor Desmond Yip, clinical haematologist Dr Nalini Pati, clinical nurse consultant Wendy Spencer and oncology pharmacist Beth Hua provided forty Solomon Islands health professionals in Honiara with a five-day training program. They then set up a medical oncology unit in the national hospital. .²⁴⁴

When Brian was in the Solomons we had a meeting and meal with Ronnie, Brian's cousin. Ronnie was gaunt and worried and urged Brian to help the family establish a business. Brian agreed, and so Makira Gold was born.

Chapter 15

MAKIRA GOLD - FROM CACAO FARMERS TO ARTISAN CHOCOLATE MAKERS

It was the second generation which finally achieved the dream of the first, the establishment of a successful business. George and his family in the Solomons attempted multiple times but never succeeded.

It was Brian, who with the same passion, patience and determination that he applied to the pilot Gardasil project, finally succeeded. He established a social enterprise called Makira Gold which supports cacao farmers in the Solomons to produce high-grade beans fit for the best markets in the world.[245] It has been a long and difficult struggle that began in 2015.

I was with Brian when we met Ronnie Maxell, his cousin, in Honiara in April that year. The cervical cancer vaccine pilot project had been launched and we invited Ronnie for a meal. Ronnie had a very poorly paid casual job which barely supported him, let alone his family back in the village. They couldn't afford school fees and clothes for the children.

Ronnie discussed starting another cleaning business in Honiara. George and I had run such a business many years earlier to supplement the income of the *Solomons Toktok*. Brian however wanted to support the villagers. He said he was more interested in cacao.

Using his own money and some borrowed from his wife's family, Brian and Ronnie began Makira Gold. Ronnie bought cacao beans in Tawatana and shipped them to Honiara. When there were enough beans, they were sold to buyers in Australia.

The traditional way of drying cacao was by using a wood fire in a dryer. It took three days, was unhealthy for the workers and resulted in smoky beans. Ronnie experimented with sun drying and solar dryers. These were not effective, particularly during overcast stormy weather. Cacao beans were also spoilt by rain or sea water when they were shipped.

Brian said he didn't realise how difficult it would be. The process of working fulltime in information technology roles in Brisbane while developing the enterprise almost sent him bankrupt. Internal sea freight costs were high, the supply of cacao beans was irregular and their quality varied. There were irregular buyers, and cashflow problems. Brian however saw the potential for high-class beans for the artisan chocolate markets and better prices for farmers.

In June 2016, he attended the first Chocolate Week

in Honiara. This was funded by the Australian Aid Program in partnership with the Adventist Relief and Development Agency (ADRA), the Pacific Horticultural and Agricultural Market Access program (PHAMA) and other representatives.

A highlight of Chocolate Week was the tasting and chocolate making process. The international chocolate makers present selected the best cacao beans from more than fifty farmers from six provinces. The top ten cacao producers then had their beans made into chocolate bars with the week ending with a final tasting and awards for the top chocolate.

At the 2016 awards ceremony, Australian High Commissioner Andrew Byrne said he was impressed by the high quality of the bars:

> Last year, some Solomon Islands cacao producers were trained in best practice fermentation and drying techniques and were able to demonstrate their skills and learn from world leading chocolate makers.[246]

The following week, the chocolate makers travelled to the provinces to visit the producers of the top ranked beans. Small quantities of cacao beans were then exported to the USA and New Zealand to be made into the first Solomon Islands single-origin chocolate bars.

In 2016, cacao was one of the Solomon Islands' biggest agricultural export earners, involving around 25,000 small holder farmers and generating around $US15 million each year.

Most of the beans were exported through the bulk market to major chocolate companies such as Nestle and Cadbury for little return. However, there was potential for better prices from niche chocolate makers.[247]

In 2016, Brian became aware of technical solutions to improve the quality of the cacao. This included the use of GrainPro products including the GrainPro solar bubble dryer and the GrainPro hermetic storage bags. The solar bubble dryer is a long, circular plastic enclosure with a zipper. There are fans at one end, fuelled by a solar battery and solar PV panels. At the other end there is a vent for the moist air. The beans take four to ten days to dry until their moisture content is an optimal 6.5 to 7.5 per cent.

The following year, 2017, Brian was back in the Solomons for Chocolate Week and travelled to Makira to establish a further partnership with his uncle, Henry Hio from Waimarae. Henry agreed to run the Makira Gold operation in Honiara.

In 2017, on the way home from a trip to Makira, Brian was at Kirakira airport waiting for the plane from Honiara when he felt sick. He vomited and then felt better. He texted Meredith and she texted back that she felt he would be all right.

He vomited again and thought it was because of a roti he had just eaten. For the next half hour he kept vomiting and began to feel worse. He walked towards the agent on the field and as he did so he collapsed. He couldn't talk.

They stopped a passing police truck and Brian was taken to the hospital. He texted Meredith and said he needed to be airlifted out. She rang back but Brian couldn't speak so gave his phone to the nurse. The nurse could only speak pidgin. I was in Darwin at that time and Meredith rang me after she had called Brian's medical insurance. They called the hospital and found he had vivax malaria. It was not considered necessary to medivac him out which was fortunate, as bad weather shut down all flights and shipping for the next three days.

During this night in hospital his 'bro', Ian Ngahu, was with him. Brian said he had never felt so sick. Every time he opened his eyes, Ian was watching him. Very sadly Ian died on 23 March 2022 from cancer. He was a very fine soccer player, a teacher, a husband and a father.

Brian was given oral antimalarials and intravenous fluids and next morning he was fine. He noticed the intravenous fluids had been donated by an organisation called the Strong Island Foundation. There were contact details. When he got back to Brisbane, he called them to thank them for supporting Kirakira Hospital and told them he had used some of their supplies.

The Strong Island Foundation was established in 2013 to improve health and education in Makira. It was founded by Dr James Fink, from Bond University. Bond University medical students have undertaken placements at Kirakira Hospital. Brian is now a board member. The foundation funds exchanges of nurses between the Gold Coast and Makira hospitals, supports the dentist and schools in Makira with materials and aids visits by Australian school parties.[248]

Brian had been taking an antimalarial, doxycycline, which does not protect against vivax malaria but does provide protection against the more dangerous non-resistant falciparum malaria. When Brian travels to Makira, he now takes a malaria testing kit and treatment.

In November 2017 Brian worked fulltime on the business for six months. It was at this time that he recruited his uncle Henry Hio from Waimarae. to run the business in the Solomons. Brian then went back to parttime work in Brisbane for the next six months.

He took this opportunity to accelerate the development of his business and ensure it was sustainable. He worked with dedicated and reliable farmers to strengthen the supply chain and ensure its reliability and quality. He instituted fermentation and drying protocols for Makira Gold farmers.

Fermentation is the first process after the beans are harvested. It kills the seeds and begins the chemical changes needed for flavour development. Boxes are used and the beans are turned daily for five or six days until they are correctly fermented and checked by using the cut test.

The beans are then either sundried or dried using a solar bubble dryer for five to ten days until the correct moisture content of 6.5 per cent is reached.

Makira Gold supplies some of their farmers on outer islands with GrainPro super grain bags to ensure their beans are protected from seawater, rain and other contaminants such as smoke.

Makira Gold farmers are paid up to twice as much as those farmers who sell to the bulk commodity market in Honiara. These high-quality beans are sold to South Pacific Cacao, a chocolate factory in Sydney which Brian owns with chocolate artisan Jessica Pedemont. Others are sold to chocolate makers in Australia such as Metiisto Chocolate in Toowoomba.

New Zealand customers include Wellington Chocolate Factory and Ocho while European customers include Fabric Chocolate, Original Beans and Macao Movement.

Brian was in the Solomons in May 2018 for the first SolChoc festival, which combined the previous Chocolate Week with public events. These were first held towards the end of the weeklong festival. Profits were channelled back to the cacao farmers.

In late 2018, Brian returned to Waimarae. He and the family had a vision of developing a cacao fermentary, research centre and cacao homestay.

They also wanted to continue with a protection plan for leatherback turtles which nest on the local beach. They formed a community cooperative, Biana Bana - which means the 'roots of Bana' in Arosi - Bana being Barnabas, Brian's great-uncle. With support by the company GrainPro, which provided a marketing specialist to travel with Brian, they produced a video called *A Farmer's Story, Continuing the Legacy* (Cristobal, 2018).

The voiceover is by Kukamwane Hiyo, Barnabas' nephew:

> Life in the Solomons has not always been easy and stable.
> There has been uncertainty and struggle
> Loss and sacrifice.
> The ethnic tension brought struggle
> Closer to the heart and culture of the Solomons
> We have had our fair share of hardships
> We do what we can
> And sometimes it is not enough
> Life is difficult and sometimes life has a different plan from what we have in mind
> My late Uncle Barnabas especially felt that
> He worked hard building ships for the Solomon Islands Shipping Services and to provide for his family
> His heart was broken when the ships he worked on were wrecked.
> But despite that, he made sure the family had something valuable
> Makira Gold not only wants to distribute cacao from the Solomon Islands.
> More importantly, it wants to be a leader of innovation
> To help farmers better manage their farms
> And adapt new technology

> And to create world class cacao.
> Biana Bana
> Meaning the children of Barnabas
> We aim to continue with Uncle Barnabas' dream.
> When Uncle Barnabas passed away
> He didn't just leave us some parcels of land
> He left his legacy to us.
> He taught us to work hard and persevere
> And endure tough times
> Our Uncle Barnabas taught us that.

The chocolate week and subsequent SolChoc festivals proved to be a successful promotion of Solomon Islands' cacao and contributed to creating new relationships and partnerships between chocolate makers and cacao producers.

After Brian met Hawaiian ethnobotanist and chocolate maker Nat Bletter during the 2016 chocolate week, Nat introduced Brian to Jessica Pedemont, one of Australia's foremost chocolate artisans.

Brian and Jessica shared the same values and passions for supporting the cacao farmers in the Pacific and after a few years of planning, launched their joint chocolate making social enterprise, South Pacific Cacao, in January 2020 with a small chocolate production and retail store in Haberfield, Sydney.

South Pacific Cacao's vision is for prosperous, connected and empowered smallholder farming communities in the South Pacific. Within a few months of opening, the COVID pandemic took hold and severely disrupted the new business. Fortunately, through perseverance and sacrifice, especially from Jessica who was running the day-to-day operations, the chocolate social enterprise survived the pandemic and business for Easter 2022 was brisk with the arrival of cacao shipments from the Solomons.

The quality of some of the Solomon Islands cacao that South Pacific Cacao uses is outstanding. Jessica, in an SBS interview on 24 September 2020, said of one farmer, David Kebu:

> He's based on Guadalcanal, he manages that farm with his extended family and six sisters. It's a 10-hectare farm that's considered quite large. He was in the top fifteen [in the Salon du Chocolat] in Paris, which is huge to be rated on that international level.

Another farmer involved is Philip Lepping. He sends his beans from Santa Cruz, the eastern most point of the Solomons and three days by boat from Honiara. He may be growing the original beans from the Spaniards, who visited the islands in the sixteenth century, although this has not been confirmed.[249]

In October and November, South Pacific Cacao sold Makira A1 fundraising packs with A1 standing for the Arosi One games due to be held in Makira later in 2021.

The money went to purchase iron goal posts for netball

Chapter 15 Makira Gold – from cacao farmers to artisan chocolate makers

courts, netball nets and soccer balls and also to complete some welding work. There is a link to an Arosi1 Facebook page with photos of the work in progress and referee training. Makira Gold also sponsored uniforms for two teams.

With the support of the Strong Island Foundation, Brian supported George from January 2019 until mid-2021 in Kirakira. George worked as a journalist writing dozens of articles about Makira that have been published in national Solomon Islands newspapers. One of George's roles was also to assist with the Makira Banana (Huki) festival. After a two-year absence, the festival was successfully held in October 2019 due to George's efforts, including acting as vice-chairperson on the organising committee.

George was living in a relative's rest home which sadly burnt down in October 2021. Fortunately no-one was injured. George was left with nothing but the clothes he stood up in and his mobile phone.

He called Brian and the Australian family was ready to provide support. When Brian called the next day, he found George was staying with the Premier, and media colleagues from Honiara held a collection and sent him several boxes of items.

A photo on Facebook taken after the fire shows George

looking frail and he told me he had suffered multiple bouts of malaria.

He has returned to Tawatana and Brian keeps in touch. In April 2021 there were thirty-five Covid cases in Tawatana but George, who is vaccinated, was not infected.

I have spoken with George about this memoir and the possibility of him writing a book. Although anthropologists, travellers and ex-residents write about the Solomons, very few Solomon Islanders do. If George is willing and well, I hope the next memoir will be his.

Chapter 16

CATCHING UP — RETURN TRIP TO THE SOLOMONS

(28 September to 9 November 2022)

Before I'd even left Australia, I was given my first update. While waiting to check in on 28 September 2022, Jennifer Anga, the head of the vaccination program in the Solomons, updated me on the Gardasil vaccination program. Although it was suspended during the covid lockdown, it had been reinstated with Dr Divi Oga Oga supervising and consultant Dr Scott La Montagne supporting him. They are considering replacing the current two dose schedule with one dose as it is almost as effective.

The next day I caught up with Rosalie Habu who also married a Solomon Islander in the seventies. She said the November riots were terrible and this was confirmed when I saw the damage and read that sixty-three buildings were burnt or looted, and $SI 44 million lost (about $A 8.3 million). In the February 2022 edition of *Island Business*, Georgina Keke reported a thousand people lost their jobs.

There was the perception that the Leader of the Opposition, Matthew Wale, may have been involved.

I was shocked by the number of new Chinese buildings, which now stretched to the airport, and dismayed by the scale of the stadiums for the South Pacific Games to be held in November 2023.

'A debt trap,' I thought glumly and wondered how long the facilities would be maintained. I had seen the crumbling remains of Chinese built facilities for a South Pacific Games in Samoa in 2009, two years after they were built.

It was a relief to fly to Makira two days later to be greeted by Rebecca, my stepdaughter. She had been up since 3am on a truck from travelling from Kanasoghu, her village, a six-hour road trip. We spent the next two days buying provisions. Every few hours George would text with another item. Finally, I replied saying I had run out of money.

On Sunday at 8 am Rebecca's uncle, her boyfriend and an assistant arrived in their canoe. They went to fill up but the depot man had lost his key. It was found, we boarded, the assistant driver yanked the starter cord – and broke it. We paddled ashore and after a further wait finally roared off and dropped Rebecca's uncle back at Kanasoghu, an hour away.

Passing Boroni the canoe began to splutter, and we limped into Hagaura. As we plodded up the beach, I heard another canoe arrive and turned around to see Henry Hio.

Henry, a mechanic and handyman, worked with Brian on Makira Gold and was now a trainer at the Boroni Rural Training Centre. He had heard the troubled canoe, looked out, saw me and followed us. He told us the gearbox was wrecked and walked across to his village to find another one.

Two hours later we left, arriving in Tawatana around 4 pm. After waiting most of the day at the beach, George had gone back up to the house. As I greeted him, I wondered if he found me as changed as I found him. He had lost weight and most of his hair and teeth, with only one front tooth remaining. His sunken cheeks were covered with fine grey hair. I was shocked by his slow mincing walk. He is in his early seventies, while I am sixty-nine. He doesn't know when he was born but accepted the birthdate in November 1953 given to him by the expatriate journalists who organised his first passport. His younger brother Peter was born in 1952.

Inside, I was overwhelmed by the empty shell of the house, the holes in the walls, and the lack of doors and privacy. The timber floor had absorbed so much dust that for the first four days I sneezed continuously. Then I fell ill with laryngitis and sinusitis.

We had a good meal that night, provided by the Mothers' Union members who each week picked an elderly person to eat with and pray for. That night, without knowing I was coming, they had picked George. They took the opportunity to warmly welcome me.

That first night I lay on a thin mattress on the floor. Any

breeze from the higher single window evaded me and the mosquito net made it even more claustrophobic. Finally, George lent me his thicker mattress and I finally slept after moving into a better ventilated room.

The next day, Eunice, George's aunt, began cleaning the rooms and a friend, Nunuau, lent me a thicker mattress, a bedsheet and pillow. Nongi, another relative, pushed a village bed through the window. At last I was level with the windows.

George was miserable when I first arrived. He was lonely. Eunice cooked for him and with Nunuau, was the only person to befriend him. George was considering an invitation by other relatives to move to South Malaita the day before I arrived. Brian asked him to stay for my visit, so he had.

In January 2022 George moved to Tawatana and had to sleep in Eunice's sago palm kitchen for three months. His brother Billy lived in the house and it took him this time to sort his things. George said when he moved in it was filthy. It took him and his niece, Alison, three days to clean the sink. The tank hadn't been cleaned for years. When I released the stop to get water to flush the toilet, the water smelt of rotten eggs. I recognised this as giardia from my Cambodian experience.

In the kitchen were the gas cooker, plates, pots and cutlery that George's media colleagues sent him after he lost everything in a rest-house fire in Kirakira in November 2021. In June 2022 Brian sent money and George hired

Chapter 16 Catching up — Return trip to the Solomons

people to plant his first crop of kumaras around the house. Before I arrived, a new septic tank had been installed and the rotten walls of the outside toilet and shower replaced. While I was there the tank was cleaned and connected to the kitchen sink.

It was a challenging environment. At night I would lie in bed and listen to the rats. George fed them so they wouldn't eat his clothes. They didn't but they gnawed on the timber and plumbing in the house. The roosters woke up at 3 or 4-am and began crowing under the house, and this woke the eighteen-month-old boy next door.

When a swarm of bees settled in my open window I protested. I am allergic to them and although I had an epi-pen I was not confident about being stung by a full swarm. George smoked them out, but the odd straggler returned. They finally left when a branch of vicious ants was placed under them.

The village water system was intermittent, and we had to coax people to carry water up to wash with. Tawatana stream has numerous houses backing on to it, and George refused to bath there, even at night, because of the lack of privacy. I wasn't strong enough to carry a bucket of water up the steep coral path and George couldn't get up it at all.

The perfect solution was found shortly before I left. Eunice persuaded her grandsons to take a suitable container with them when they went for their wash. The ten-year-old took a small bucket, while the youngest, the four-year-old, had a small bottle. The five boys then carried up their containers and tipped them into our bucket. I finally saw the positive side of having a large family.

One night I woke up to find a gale and fine rain driving through my open window. I pulled back the mattress and unsuccessfully tried to hook the flimsy curtain in place. Giving up sleep I watched the violently swaying palms and recollected one had fallen and destroyed a previous verandah. In the morning George pointed out more than six trees that threatened the house. I emailed Brian to remind him.

Slowly George became reconciled to retirement. He begged me to take his photo when he planted twenty mounds of kumaras with a borrowed hoe. He enjoyed the birdlife which was returning after logging; the fantails, the doves, the frigate birds and the solitary white heron he saw. He took an interest in two orphaned chickens which he said were the remainder of a brood of ten, neglected by the hen. We put them under cover at night, but a hawk finally got them.

He spent most of his time in the house because he didn't know many of the villagers and they didn't know him. He had left the village when he was eleven and only returned for short visits.

It was extraordinary George left the village because his other siblings didn't. He had a rocky start. He was expelled from Tawatana school by the headmaster when he was ten for poor attendance and for being a 'big head'. He stayed with his grandparents, Sahu and Oageni, for three months. When the entry test for Waimapuru, a senior primary school, was sent to class two students at Tawatana, his class teacher asked the headmaster if George could sit it. He was given permission and was first in English. He was then accepted for Waimapuru, and after attending a series of boarding schools went on to complete form three. He was accepted by the government information and broadcasting department as a cadet journalist in 1972.

He continued as a journalist and then in 2003, during the ethnic tension, thought it safer to work with the government. He became Prime Minister Alan Kemakeza's press secretary. After hearing the Prime Minister and his senior advisors discussing an invitation to Indonesia for assistance, George wrote a press release that day, Monday, which was broadcast worldwide. The Australian Prime Minister, John Howard, who had been asked first and declined, changed his mind on Wednesday and RAMSI was born.

We both slowly recuperated, and after a course of antibiotics I felt better and began to explore. When George could accompany me, he did, but as he couldn't walk far Eunice and Nunuau were often my companions and teachers.

The village was crowded now. Because of the big families there was little family land available for business. The coconuts in the plantation, which George's father Basil had planted to fund his children's education, were being eaten by the villagers. Ida, George's sister, took me up to the gardens and showed me the stunted cassavas and small kumaras produced when the land was not allowed to remain fallow for at least two years. People went further to the more fertile land which had lain unused for at least ten years. Ida taught me that if bananas grew the fertility was okay.

Money had become more important. The community school with its twenty-eight teachers (seventeen of them secondary) drove the village economy. In late October 2022 there were 621 students with fifty in early learning and the rest spread between the primary and secondary sections. Many of the secondary students secured a place in a national secondary school. The younger children spoke and learnt in Arosi before graduating to pidgin and English.

Each school day a band of market ladies would assemble before 7.30 am and stay until after the break between 10 am and 10.30 am. School fees for secondary students ranged from $SI 1000 to $SI 1500 depending on whether they boarded. This made saving imperative and the Mothers' Union ran their own savings club while World Vision supported village savings clubs.

There are not enough jobs for graduates because of the high growth rate of 2.7 per cent (2019 census), the highest in the Pacific.

Many youths dropped out and some become addicted to cannabis, kwaso (illegal alcohol) and sex, all of which were readily available. As in Australia, some of the cannabis users became psychotic as I witnessed in Ubuna.

While I was in Tawatana the psychiatrist Dr Paul Orotaloa held a two-day workshop at the school for the teachers about youth and mental health. He suggested if teachers were concerned they should send students to the clinic. Keithford Maitoro, a nurse at the Heraniau clinic, has psychiatric training and experience and can assess and refer patients.

Modern life may have affected people in other ways. Twenty years ago, George and I agreed, there seemed few elderly people with dementia. His parents and uncles and aunts didn't experience it. Now Eunice said there were six or more currently affected or who had recently died. Ester's husband, George, was one of them. Four years ago she noticed the symptoms and since then has rarely been out of his earshot. She no longer keeps a garden. Her children provide for them both, and she continues to cook.

George looked like an Old Testament prophet as he pointed at me, proclaiming the same sentence about God over and over. "Finally, Ester said 'Sleep' and he did". She said he loved looking at the stream and trees beside his mattress. He always looked cheerful.

Another reaction to modern life has been to flee from it. Two days before I left, I met Georgina Oroi from the Platform Movement. She advanced looking guilty. She was a teacher, and I knew about the movement's stance which did not permit western education, western medicine or western religion. I smiled at her and, emboldened, she asked for stationery and drawing material for the men's art class.

Her brothers Andrew and Peter convinced others to settle in the bush in 2011 and since then Georgina, another sister and their mother have joined them. There are more than a hundred people in their group and there are about ten of these groups throughout the Makira/Ulawa province. After a stroke Georgina's mother Mary returned to Tawatana but insisted on going back to the bush, telling Eunice she expected a big payout. After ten years it hasn't happened, and people are beginning to filter back to the coast.

Charlie, George's brother, was up in the bush at Platform with his wife and some of their children when he got sick. Charlie has never believed in school and few of his ten children are literate.

We got word that Charlie hadn't eaten or drunk for five or six days and was coughing. Betty and Rosa, two of his nieces went up and Betty told him she wasn't going to leave until he did. A group of Platform members carried him down and he was then carried by the family to the clinic.

I went to see him and didn't recognise him. He had been tall and muscular and now he was a frail gnome with black woolly hair and a wispy grey beard. His legs were wasted and folded under him and he said he was unable to walk. He wanted soap and sweet biscuits, so I went to buy them, supervised by his daughter.

Jane, the nurse at Ubuna, said he was virtually semiconscious when he arrived, and his chest was full of fluid. She immediately started him on IV Amoxycillin and he slowly recovered and began to eat and drink again. After a few weeks a house on the family land was prepared for him and he and his family came back to live in the village. He sent round a sweet bunch of bananas one morning.

I was surprised when the nurses at both Ubuna and Heraniau told me that during the last two years there had been an increased uptake of a progesterone implant Jadelle, which lasts for five years. Jane had almost fifty clients and Masey at Heraniau, thirty.

The number of deliveries at Ubuna had dropped from twelve to fourteen a month to one or two. Deliveries at Heraniau had also dropped. At last it seemed the women were adopting family planning.

Both clinics were old. Ubuna clinic was twenty-seven years old, the roof leaked, the tank had been removed and rust was visible. A replacement was planned but not being built. Heraniau, which had been built by the Seventh Day Adventists, was termite affected with some rooms unusable. They did a few deliveries, but with no autoclave available, had to wash everything thoroughly and put them in the sun. The women did not get postnatal infections.

Neither clinic had access to a canoe. Keithford said as well as being useful for emergencies, a canoe would assist with holding clinics in villages for outpatients, antenatal clients, baby checks, carrying out vaccinations and giving health talks. She said they had had a two-month malaria outbreak with a hundred cases in Maranu'u which had finally resolved. The malaria team had visited and given out impregnated bed nets while she held health talks about prevention, including clearing bushes and burying rubbish.

It is no longer infectious diseases which kill most Solomon Islanders but noncommunicable diseases such as diabetes, heart disease, cancer and chronic lung disease. Almost one in five people in the Solomons now has diabetes and it is listed by WHO among the top fifteen countries.

Many Solomon Islanders now eat a lot of white rice. I witnessed this on a sixteen-hour boat trip between Tawatana and Kirakira in early November on the ship the *Fair Chief*. The trip takes three hours by canoe. It took so long because every village and school along the coast received multiple dinghy-loads of rice, flour and sugar. In Tawatana we boarded at 10 am and waited for two hours as the dinghy went back and forward before the ship finally left.

I was horrified when I saw an advertisement along the road to the airport in Honiara saying solrais, (pidgin for Solomon Island rice) is good for you. As the Tikopian pastor who watched the loading with me for part of the journey said, 'That food is killing us.' And neither is it Solomon Island rice. All the rice is imported and repackaged.

There is a network of twelve provincial NCD coordinators who treat patients, but the health message doesn't seem to be getting through. Many women sell their sweet potatoes and cabbage, coconuts and pawpaws to buy rice.

One man who was maintaining a traditional food source was village chief Ben Aharo. I met him going up and down hills, his knee bandage in place, carrying buckets of food for his pigs. One day he agreed to sit down with me and update me on logging in Tawatana.

He said another wave of logging that began in 2016 was even more divisive than the logging I witnessed in 2006. The Ocean Trading Company, logging in Ubuna under the licence of the Triple A Holding Company, was invited into Tawatana by three landowners.

On 4 November 2016, as the first logging truck began to cross the Boda into Tawatana, the head ranger, Homeless, also known as Alfred Thomas Hill, fired a ship's rocket towards them. He was arrested and charged the next day and placed on a good behaviour bond for two years. Two days later loggers assaulted Monty, another ranger, knocking him to the ground. The other two rangers were assaulted early in 2017. Although complaints were made to the police no action was taken.

Ben said although the logging company began on land they had consent for, they then moved on to land that had not been consented.

On 19 January 2017 Ben established the boundaries of the Ameo tribe with the Council of Chiefs and then approached the Public Solicitor's Office requesting a review of the logging process.

The matter then went to the High Court which did not make a ruling but instead asked the complainant to pay expenses of $SI 45,000 within thirty days if the case was to proceed. The case was dropped. There was a dispute about the land rights versus timber rights.

Danny Vaka, the forestry officer in Kirakira, explained that some of Ben's brothers supported logging, while others did not. They all owned the land, and all had equal say in the timber rights. If the brothers who supported logging consented, they had a right to do so. The High Court decision sent the matter back to the family to sort out themselves.

On 4 April 2017, Ben set fire to a forestry excavator he said was trespassing. The case was heard in the Kirakira court in July 2017 and Ben was acquitted. However, logging continued in Tawatana until 22 May 2019.

During 2006 we also attempted to interrupt the logging and I had hoped we succeeded. However, Danny Vaka told me the logging company Yankin Baiyan continued until 2008. Logging recommenced in 2010 with the licence still held by the provincial member, Peter Baewai, with the logging company now Ocean Express. Logging then stopped in 2013 before restarting in 2016.

I asked Danny Vaka about replanting. He said planting of teak, mahogany and melaena had occurred on a small scale, with most plantations being one to two hectares, with the largest six. The reforestation unit of the forestry department supported the projects. One company, KPL, applied for an export licence for teak but had yet to hear the outcome. Teak can be milled at ten years.

Danny said the most sustainable solution was to encourage the regrowth of the native tree, akwa, Logging was still going ahead in the middle island and at the same time the landowners were protecting and tending their stands of akwa, which is not a hardwood but can be used for houses and furniture.

Danny also advised me about the protected area that Ben had told me about. Ben said he and his son Selwyn founded the Tawatana Community Conservation Development Association (TCCDA) in 2014. With World Vision the association aimed to register 4,000 hectares in the high bush, all owned by the Ameo tribe, as a protected area. World Vision was supporting them to hold a hearing on 15 and 16 November in Tawatana to finalise the process.

All three Makira endemic bird species had been identified in the area by Dr Maeni, botanist from the Honiara Botanical Gardens. They include a ground dwelling pigeon, a local honeyeater and a large cuckoo.

Before I left I walked to Ubuna to see Alick, also known as Saro, Rebi's brother and the chief of our family.

He told me he had looked after Haruta, built a new sago palm hut and kitchen and lived with him until he died. I was glad to hear this because when I last saw Haruta he was living under a collapsed shelter. Saro also cared for John Tarodo, my bush guide. Like his brother Hoa before him, Saro had not agreed to logging on the family land.

Saro said his generation had been hard working and business minded, and pointed to Basil and Barnabas as examples. Barnabas bought and was given plots of land around the Solomons which his family is still catching up with. I agreed the middle generation, George and his siblings, had shown little business acumen. However, I disagreed about the new generation and pointed to Brian (Makira Gold) and John Wesley, whose financial acumen had renewed the Anglican Church in Makira and was now benefiting Tawatana school.

I also acknowledged Selwyn Aharo, Ben's son, who trained as a teacher and then returned to the village, starting a store, a fuel depot, a liquor shop and now, a rest house.

Saro also spoke of how the big families meant that land, even in the bush, was now scarce. He said the bush from Ubuna down to Marou Bay was now full and when I flew over from Kirakira I saw this. He also said there were social problems in Marou Bay, with big cannabis plantations and kwaso (illegal spirits) manufacture. He said the public believed that the police did not uproot the plantations as they were involved.

I put this to a member of the provincial government.

He looked at me sadly and said, 'Everyone is corrupt, the chiefs, the politicians, the public servants, the police.' Uncharacteristically I was speechless.

Silas Tawa, the village chief, was very concerned by the lawlessness there and George was helping him find assistance to renovate the Melanesian Brothers' house in

Marou Bay. As before in the Solomons the Brothers are called in when civil society fails.

Another thing that saddened me in Tawatana was the lack of books, hymn books, service books and bibles.

In 2004, when Daphne and Roger Kahler came to witness Brian and Meredith's marriage there were books including children's books. One of the girls was named after Daphne and grew up reading. She had just sat a trial exam to enter Form 3 and got 94 out of 100 for English. She is expected to be attend a national secondary school next year.

When I shook hands with many children at my farewell, wishing them well, Eunice introduced one boy, about eight, who went around picking up pieces of paper, trying to teach himself to read. The school has a library, but the books are difficult to access even for students.

Eunice and Ida, executives from the Mothers' Union books held a meeting with the majority of members requesting support for books for a community library. I took the minutes along with a letter to the Mothers' Union executive in Honiara. The vice-president, Sandra, said she hoped to visit them in the new year. I would like to help identify suitable books in Australia, but have yet to establish a means of transport.

In Kirakira library the books were out of date and irrelevant. Chief education officer Gilbert Tabihau agreed, and said the books sent were worthless. I also spoke with Olive Suaro, a retired nurse with many skills including cooking, sewing, weaving and running a business. She agreed her friends with secretarial and editing skills could create booklets for those with lower literacy.

It wasn't until I was in Kirakira speaking with forestry officer Danny Vaka that I realised the significance of Saro's decision to ban logging on the family land.

Danny Vaka said 2,000 hectares of virgin bush had been saved and international birdwatchers, including an Italian group, had travelled to Tawatana to see it.

In Kirakira I bumped into two Europeans, one with a large camera. They were Kevin and Wojciech of Bird Explorers iNaturalist, based in Fiji. They were escorted by their friend, Charles Tatahu, a writer, poet and librarian from Central Bauro. When I spoke of Tawatana they were interested and wanted to know about the access. I have discussed this with Brian who will be visiting the Solomons with Meredith and their three children in June 2023.

They said the biodiversity in Makira was quite extraordinary and included not only birds, but marine life and many kinds of animals and insects.

I also spoke with Charles about Father Abel Ta'ais' work, which his son, Cyril Dadama, a science teacher at Tawatana, is compiling. Charles agreed it was a remarkable record of life in the bush. In the unlogged areas around Tawatana it is still possible to see the old villages.

Father Abel wrote that he could only know himself if he understood how his ancestors lived and thought. This drove him to interview old people in the sixties and seventies when oral history and bush knowledge were still available. Much of it has gone now.

Whatever the difficulties in Makira, people have more chance to chart their own course.

In Honiara I met Gilbert and told him I was stopping to take a photo of the word sad on an appropriately blue wall. He agreed and left me, while behind a woman screamed at a man in pidgin. 'Don't ask me for money. Go and get a job.'

I'm sure he has tried. There are very few jobs.

I look at these crowds around me and wonder how they live. Perhaps they sell a few betel nuts, a few cigarettes, find bottles in the trash, wander around, crashing with relatives and sleeping on the streets.

Chinese development benefits a favoured few. Let's hope other donor countries, including our own, can do better.

Finale

On my return, I found a poem I wrote for my two sons in Wellington in December 1986. Brian was seven and John five. It encapsulates my feelings about the Solomons and my sons'. It is their heritage. My time in the Solomons is almost over.

I know not what echoes sound through your minds.
Echoes of silent, dark races.
A sentinel
stands in the moonlight
on some great plateau
watching.

But in the day you are as quick as lynxes,
body flashing,
mind untarnished,
many faceted – glittering,
reflecting, questioning,
seeking the ore,
the rock on which to rest.

And you ask me of your father,

but you will not listen.
'No,' you say,
'I have no father.'

All right.
So your father is the wind,
blowing through that great land
which gave you birth.
And the proud strong men paddling
were just a shadow.
A breath on the water.

But you emerge from the elements,
that many bloodied mix
and straddling it
stand firm and free.

AFTERWORD

BY GEORGE ATKIN

What attracted me to Margaret was her great curiosity. This curiosity equipped her to settle into a very different culture, and later drove her as a journalist.

After we married in 1976, she returned to NZ to get further nursing experience and qualifications and I joined her. Firstly, I missed her and secondly, Chief Minister Solomon Mamaloni advised me, through the senior government information officer, that I was to either follow the government line or leave. I left because I believe in a free press. I decided when we returned, I would start an independent newspaper.

Margaret and I have been concerned about the high birth-rate since pre-independence and she raises this. Sadly, the Solomons has sleepwalked into a situation that was predicted many years ago. This includes unemployment, social breakdown, and pressure on natural resources and social services such as health and education. In many areas including Tawatana, where I am now living, there are shortages of land, fish and timber. This will lead to further urban drift and reliance on imported food.

In 1982, when the Prime Minister Solomon Mamaloni gave the government paper, the *Solomons News Drum*, to my former colleagues I was upset. However, I understood. Because I was his cousin, he did not want to be accused of nepotism. John Lemani, the editor, was fortunate to have the late Imo Ta'asi as his lead writer. He had a talent for finding great stories.

Margaret remains concerned about the situation of women in the Solomons including the high rate of domestic violence. Some of this is alcohol fuelled but I think the cultural practice of paying a 'bride price' also contributes. As the woman has been bought the purchaser may feel he can treat her however he chooses.

The status of women is slowly changing. In Isabel there is now a female premier, and in Honiara when the wife makes more money than her husband, she commonly runs the household finances. The Family Act (2015-2016) ensures both men and women can take family members to court if they experience domestic violence.

The day Margaret and the children left the Solomons on 7 February 1984 was one of the saddest in my life.

The four of us went to town. We bought the boys ice-creams and then split up at the market. In the evening I got home and found they weren't there. I looked into every bus and taxi, but they still didn't arrive.

Finally, I went to see Jane and her husband. They told

me they had left. I broke down and went to Prime Minister Mamaloni's house, which was nearby.

He too was surprised.

'Oh yeah?' he said.

Reflecting on our separation now I realise how difficult it can be for a husband and wife to work together. I realise I should have asked Margaret to handle the money much earlier. I also didn't realise how much Gill and Ray contributed. I knew they had given money for the building, but I was so busy working I didn't think about it.

Margaret's reflections after she left include the incident when a cabinet minister was jailed and then permitted to attend cabinet meetings. There was widespread anger about this.

That decision was overturned and subsequently it was acknowledged that no one is above the law. That was evident during 2002 and 2003, during the tension, when the Prime Minister Alan Kemakeza was imprisoned.

I know about my grandfather Sahu's imprisonment, but I had not heard about the murder of the European. I suspect this may have been the plantation manager employed by Levers at Marou Bay. Frederick Campbell subsequently bought the plantation with others along the West Makira Coast.

Our mutual love and respect was evident when Margaret returned with our sons in 1992. Despite the perception I would soon get another partner, I didn't live with another woman until 1999. That was Kate, my son

Harry's mother. Harry was born in 2003 and we separated after that. I found it strange to hear another small boy calling me 'Daddy.'

When Margaret returned to the Solomons in 1998 to investigate the cervical cancer situation Brian and I met her in Tawatana. We arrived on the *Ocean Express*. It was a terrible voyage. The rough weather continued, and the ship sank on its return trip, off Guadalcanal, with no loss of life.

When Margaret and Alick walked downtown on 20 April 2006 to the wharf they didn't realise that in nearby Commonwealth Avenue a fuel depot was burning. It was very dangerous. I was advised by RAMSI not to go back to my house in Chinatown. I spent the next two weeks in the RAMSI house.

The school and community education programs Margaret carried out in 2006 with the support of Mothers' Union and Save the Children volunteers are like those I would like to hold for other topics. The radio reception is poor and rural education sessions by the province have been affected by budget constraints. I hope to hold sessions on the Land Reform Act and village and market hygiene.

When Margaret asked me why AIDS never became the problem here it was in PNG, I said it was because the people were less promiscuous and more receptive to education.

After I lost my job as research officer for the opposition leader Dr Derek Sikua in 2012 I was homeless for a year. I ended up sleeping at the Central Bank. There was a very

AFTERWORD *by George Atkin*

kind security guard from North Malaita who laid down cardboard for me to sleep on. Since then, I have been more tolerant of North Malaitans. During the tension they saved my life on several occasions.

I am proud of Brian's business, Makira Gold, and agree my generation have tried and failed with business set-ups. I hope this will change.

I intend to write my memoirs and see my retirement in Tawatana as an opportunity to do this. I have been a journalist and political insider for most of my working life and they will be full and frank.

Bibliography

ACCF. (2021). https://accf.org.au/about-us/international-programs/solomon-islands/. Retrieved from https://accf.org.au.

ACCF. (2020, May). https://accf.org.au/a-decade-of-making-a-difference/. Retrieved from https://accf.org.au.

Angiki, D. (2009, June 26). https://www.solomontimes.com/letter/1958. Retrieved from https://www.solomontimes.com.

Atkin, B. October 2021. https://makiragold.com/my-story/. Retrieved from https://makiragold.com/.

Atkin, G. (2020, April 27). https://blogs.griffith.edu.au/asiainsights/. Retrieved from https://blogs.griffith.edu.au/asiainsights/finding-and-reporting-news-in-solomon-islands-the-early-days/

Atkin M. (1999). Cervical Cancer in the Solomon Islands - A Pilot Study. Cervical Cancer in the Solomon Islands - A Pilot Study. Brisbane, Queensland, Australia: Unpublished.

Australian High Commission, Solomon Islands. 8 June 2016. https://solomonislands.highcommission.gov.au/honi/080616.html. Retrieved from https://solomonislands.highcommission.gov.au.

Australian Institute of Health and Welfare. (1996). https://www.aihw.gov.au/getmedia/cae88d96-857b-4c84-ab5a-10ead6e2a908/bccsa96-7-c03.pdf.aspx. Retrieved from https://www.aihw.gov.au/.

Australian National University, Globilisation and Governance in the Pacific Islands, Conference, October 2005, https://pressfiles.anu.edu.au/downloads/press/p55871/mobile/ch12s02.html

Barett P. S. (1996). Cervical Cytology Registry of Western Australia 1996 Statistical Report. Perth: Health Department of Western Australia.

Brown, T. (2018). The Solomon Islands, 'Ethnic Tension' Conflict and the Solomon Islands Truth and Reconciliation Commission: A Personal Reflection. In D. Webster, Flowers in the Wall: Truth and Reconciliation in Timor-Leste, Indonesia, and Melanesia (pp. pp 279-292). Calgary: University of Calgary.

Canfell, K. (2017, January 9). https://www.cancercouncil.com.au/news/australian-success-story-hpv-vaccine/. Retrieved from https://www.cancercouncil.com.au.

Cristobal, G. (2018, November 11). https://makiragold.com/2019/05/10/biana-bana/. Retrieved from https://makiragold.com.

Dan, G. (23 May 2014). https://www.lowyinstitute.org/the-interpreter/interpreters-best-2014-modi-ramsi-obama-west-point-and-mosul-falls. Retrieved from https://www.lowyinstitute.org/the-interpreter/.

Fiji Pine Commission, https://fijipine.com.fj/about-us/mission-vision-and-objectives/ Undated, Retrieved 17 March 2022.

Family Planning NSW. (2021, October). https://www.fpnsw.org.au/international/solomonislands. Retrieved from https://www.fpnsw.org.au.

Fiji Pine Commission, Accessed April 2022, https://fijipine.com.fj/about-us/mission-vision-and-objectives/

Fraenkel J, 2005, The Manipulation of Custom, From Uprising to Intervention in the Solomon Islands, New Ed, Pandanus Press Originally published 2004.

Fraenkel J, 29 April 2019, East Asia Forum, The politics of riots in the Solomon Islands https://fraenkel49.rssing.com/chan-39261217/article9.html

Frazer 1997 in Kabutaulaka T. Chapter 12, Solomon Islands Forestry and local ownership in Chapter 12, of Australian National University Conference, Globalisation and Governance in the Pacific Islands, October 2005, https://press-files.anu.edu.au/downloads/press/p55871/pdf/book.pdf

Griffith Asia Institute. (2020, April 27). https://blogs.griffith.edu.au/asiansights/finding-and-reporting-news-in-solomon-islands-the-early-days/. Retrieved from https://blogs.griffith.edu.au/asiansights/.

Kalinga Senevirante, 22 April 2006, InterPress Service South Pacific fear of domination sparked anti-chinese riots https://www.ipsnews.net/2006/04/south-pacific-fear-of-domination-sparked-anti-chinese-riots/

Karen, C. (2017, January 9). https://www.cancercouncil.com.au/news/australian-success-story-hpv-vaccine/. Retrieved from https://www.cancercouncil.com.au.

Lam, L. T. (2020, September 24).. https://www.sbs.com.au/food/article/2020/09/24/chocolate-changes-lives-solomon-islands. Retrieved from https://www.sbs.com.au/.

Latu, J. (2010, March 17). https://pacific.scoop.co.nz/2010/03/solomon-islands-women-barrier-breakers-tell-their-stories/. Retrieved from https://pacific.scoop.co.nz.

Masalai-i-tokout.com, 45, 27 April 2006, The untold story- the Solomons, Logging corruption ruins a nation, https://pngforests.files.wordpress.com/2014/02/masalai-45-the-role-of-forestry-corruption-in-the-solomons-crisis.pdf

Maukera R and Muga F, Use of tobacco, alcohol and marihuana amongst high school students in Honiara, 5th November 2018, accessed from https://az659834.vo.msecnd.net/eventsairaueprod/production-ashm-public/d2c62ac4c1714809b19ade8d0402cb5a in November 2021.

Ministry of Health and Medical Services. (1996). 1996 Review of Health Services in the Solomon Islands. Honiara: Solomon Islands Government.

Moore, C. (2013). http://www.solomonencyclopaedia.net/biogs/E000131b.htm. Retrieved from http://www.solomonencyclopaedia.net/.

New South Wales Family Planning NSWFP, 2020 Cervical Screening in the Solomon Islands | Family Planning NSW (fpnsw.org.au)

New South Wales Family Planning NSWFP Undated Solomon Islands | Family Planning NSW (fpnsw.org.au)

Noonan, S. (2020, October 27). https://www.rhdaustralia.org.au/what-acute-rheumatic-fever. Retrieved from https://www.rhdaustralia.org.au.

Office of the Auditor General. (2005). Media Statement,. Honiara: Solomon Islands Government.

Pedemont, J. (2021, October). https://www.chocolateartisan.com.au/biography. Retrieved from https://www.chocolateartisan.com.au/.

Poten J. et al. HPV and Cervical Cancer, *International Journal of Cancer*, p 317, Vol 63 Issue 2, 9 October 1995 https://doi.org/10.1002/ijc.2910630229

Royal Australasian College of Physicians (RACP). (2018, October). https://www.racp.edu.au/about/international-strategy/racp-fellow-stories/canberra-cancer-experts-enhancing-care-in-the-solomon-islands. Retrieved from https://www.racp.edu.au/.

Roughan, J. (1993). Comment John Roughan. *Solomon Voice*, 3.

Scott, M. (2021). How the Missionary got his Mana: Chares Elliot Fox and the Power of Name-Exchange in Solomon Islands. Oceania, 106-127.

Sol Choc. (2021). http://www.findglocal.com/SB/

Honiara/2054381091255825/SolChoc. Retrieved from http://www.findglocal.com/SB/Honiara/.

Solomon Islands Government. (1978). God save our Solomon Islands, Independence Souvenir Issue, *News Drum*, 1-34.

Solomon Times. (2021, October 20). https://www.solomontimes.com/news/only-12-of-target-population-vaccinated/11181. Retrieved from https://www.solomontimes.com/.

South Pacific Cacao. (2021, October). https://southpacificcacao.com/our-story/. Retrieved from https://southpacificcacao.com/.

Spiller Penny, 21 April 2006, Riots Highlight Chinese Tensions, BBC News

http://news.bbc.co.uk/2/hi/asia-pacific/4930994.stm

Strong Island Foundation. (2021). http://www.strongislandfoundation.com.au/about-2/. Retrieved from http://www.strongislandfoundation.com.au.

Ta'aimaesiburu, F. A. (1983, January 5). The story of Sahu. (M. Atkin, Interviewer)

UNDP, Solomon Islands Youth Status Report, 2018, https://www1.undp.org/content/dam/fiji/docs/UNDP-SOI-Youth-Status-Report-2018.pdf. Retrieved 17 March 2022

Unknown. (2006, April 27). https://pngforests.files.wordpress.com/2014/02/masalai-45-the-role-of-forestry-corruption-in-the-solomons-crisis.pdf. Retrieved from www.masalai-i-tokout.com.

Westoby J.C., Thomson A.P. and Leslie A.J. Solomon Islands Forest Service Organisation Study, Food and Agriculture Organisation 1976.

WHO 2017, https://www.who.int/malaria/publications/country-profiles/profile_slb_en.pdf

WHO (2019, September). https://apps.who.int/iris/handle/10665/329299. Retrieved from https://apps.who.int.

WHO (2020, August). https://www.who.int/initiatives/

cervical-cancer-elimination-initiative. Retrieved from https://www.who.int/.

WHO. (2021, May 13). https://www.who.int/news-room/feature-stories/detail/addressing-ncds-in-solomon-islands. Retrieved from https://www.who.int/.

WHO Western Pacific. (2018, August 30). https://www.who.int/news/item/30-08-2018-protecting-women-in-solomon-islands-from-cervical-cancer. Retrieved from https://www.who.int/news/item/.

World Health Organisation. (2021). https://www.who.int/data/. Retrieved from https://www.who.int/data/gho/data/themes/hiv-aids.

World Health Organisation. (2006). https://www.who.int/hiv/mediacentre/11-Oceania_2006_EpiUpdate_. Retrieved from https://www.who.int/hiv/mediacentre/.

World Obesity Organisation 2021, with data from the International Diabetes Federation, 2021. https://data.worldobesity.org/downloader/680ec04fb0cbc25c2fe76ac0fd580e75.pdf

Endnotes

Preface

1. Atkin G. The Birth of a Nation, Solomons Toktok, 7 July 1978, p 1-28
2. Atkin M, Letter to Ray and Gill Lycette 20 October 1982
3. Atkin M, Overpopulation worries Sir Peter Kenilorea, Solomons Toktok, 20 Jan 1983
4. Atkin M. Depo-provero safe to use, Solomons Toktok 17 Feb 1983, p1
5. UNDP https://www1.undp.org/content/dam/fiji/docs/UNDP-SOI-Youth-StatusReport2018.pdf. Retrieved 17 March 2022 UNDP, Solomon Islands Youth Report, 2018, p16
6. Unknown Rumble in the Jungle Chapter Six from https://press-files.anu.edu.au/downloads/press/p99101/html/ch06s02.html
    Retrieved 17 March 2022 Fraser 1997:51
7. Westoby J.C., Thomson A.P. and Leslie A.J. Forest Service Organisation Study Food and Agriculture Organisation 1976
8. https://fijipine.com.fj/about-us/mission-vision-and-objectives/ Fiji Pine Commission, Undated, Retrieved 17 March 2022
9. Atkin M, Women's Corner, Mi Mere, Solomons Toktok, 17 November 1983, p 8
10. World Obesity Org, 2021, from International Diabetes Federation 2021, see Bibliography

Chapter 1

11. Atkin M, Letter to Ray and Gill Lycette parents, 16 December 1975
12. Atkin M, Letter to Ray and Gill Lycette parents, 25 December 1975
13. Atkin M, Diary 30 December 1975
14. Atkin M, Letter to Ray and Gill Lycette, 5 Jan 1976
15. Atkin M, Letter to Ray and Gill Lycette, 11 Jan 1976
16. Atkin M, Letter to Eve and Jack Prendergast, paternal aunt, 12 Jan 1976
17. Atkin M, Letter to Ray and Gill Lycette, 14 Jan 1976
18. Atkin M, Letter to Ray and Gill Lycette, 12 Feb 1976
19. Atkin M, Letter to Ray and Gill Lycette, mid-Feb 1976

Chapter 2
20 Atkin M, Letter to Ray and Gill Lycette, 6 Nov 1977
21 Atkin G, https://blogs.griffith.edu.au/asiansights/ , 2020). Retrieved February 2022
22 Atkin, M, Letter to Ray and Gill Lycette, 14 Feb 1978
23 Atkin M, Letter to Ray and Gill Lycette, 14 Feb 1978
24 Atkin M, Letter to Ray and Gill Lycette, 4 March 1978
25 Atkin M, Letter to Ray and Gill Lycette, 22 March 1978, postmarked Malu'u Postal Agency
26 Atkin M, Letter to Ray and Gill Lycette, 7 April 1978, postmarked Bita'ama Postal Agency
27 Atkin M, Letter to Ray and Gill Lycette, 7 April 1978, postmarked Bita'ama Postal Agency
28 Atkin M, Letter to Ray and Gill Lycette, 12 April 1978
29 Atkin M, Letter to Ray and Gill Lycette, 12 April, 1978
30 Atkin M, Letter to Ray and Gill Lycette, 15 April, 1978
31 Atkin M, Letter to Ray and Gill Lycette, 26 April, 1978
32 Atkin M, Letter to Ray and Gill Lycette 8 May, 1978
33 Atkin M. Letter to Ray and Gill Lycette 22 May 1978
34 Atkin M, Letter to Ray and Gill Lycette 4 June 1978
35 Atkin M, Letter to Ray and Gill Lycette 15 June 1978
36 Atkin M, Letter to Ray and Gill Lycette, 3 July 1978
37 Atkin M, Letter to Ray and Gill Lycette 5 July 1978
38 Atkin G, The Birth of a Nation 7 July 1978, p 1-28
39 Atkin G., The Birth of a Nation 7 July 1978, p 1-28
40 Atkin M, Letter to Ray and Gill Lycette, 8 July 1978
41 Atkin M, Letter to Ray Lycette, 28 July 1978

Chapter 3
42 Atkin M Letter to Gill and Ray Lycette 25 August 1978
43 Atkin M, Letter to Gill and Ray Lycette 30 Sept 1978
44 Atkin M Letter to Gill and Ray Lycette, 24 October 1978
45 Atkin G., Solair Disaster - Pilot unable to see Bellona Solomons Toktok 4 April 1979
46 Atkin M Letter to Gill and Ray Lycette 9 November 1978
47 Atkin M, Letter to Gill and Ray Lycette, 16 November 1978
48 Atkin M Letter to Gill and Ray Lycette 24 November 1978
49 Atkin M Letter to Gill and Ray Lycette, 20 December 1978
50 Atkin G., Editor Sedition Case acquitted, Solomons Toktok January 1979
51 Atkin M Letter to Gill and Ray Lycette, 16January 1979
52 Atkin M Letter to Gill and Ray Lycette, 2 Feb 1979
53 Atkin M Letter to Gill and Ray Lycette 27 Feb 1979

54 Atkin M Letter to Gill and Ray Lycette Letter 9 March 1979
55 Atkin G, Cyclone havoc on Makira/Ulawa Province, Solomons Toktok, 14 March 1979, p 8
56 Atkin M Letter to Gill and Ray Lycette, 18 March 1979
57 Atkin M, Letter to Gill and Ray Lycette, 13 April 1979
58 Atkin M, Letter to Gill and Ray Lycette, 21 April 1979
59 Atkin M, Letter to Gill and Ray Lycette, 7 May 1979

Chapter 4
60 Atkin M, Letter to Ray and Gill Lycette, 20 May 1979
61 Atkin M, Letter to Ray and Gill Lycette, 22 May 1979
62 Atkin M, Letter to Ray and Gill Lycette, 1 June 1979
63 Atkin G, '$65,000 of goods lost in the SISCO disaster' Solomons Toktok, 18 July 1979, Front page
64 Atkin M, Letter to Ray and Gill Lycette, 9 August 1979
65 Atkin M, Letter to Ray and Gill Lycette, 18 August 1979
66 Atkin M, Letter to Ray and Gill Lycette, 7 October 1979
67 Atkin M, Letter to Ray and Gill Lycette, 23 November 1979
68 Atkin M, Letter to Ray and Gill Lycette, 16 December 1979
69 Atkin M, Letter to Ray and Gill Lycette, 29 December 1979
70 Atkin M, Letter to Ray and Gill Lycette, 13 of Jan 1980
71 Atkin M, Letter to Ray and Gill Lycette, 13 Feb 1980
72 Atkin M, Letter to Ray and Gill Lycette, 24 Feb 1980
73 Atkin M, Letter to Ray and Gill Lycette, 6 March 1980
74 Atkin M, Letter to Ray and Gill Lycette, 13 March 1980
75 Atkin M, Letter to Ray and Gill Lycette, 29 March 1980
76 Atkin M, Letter to Ray and Gill Lycette, 28 April 1980
77 Atkin M, Letter to Ray and Gill Lycette, 4 May 1980
78 Atkin M, Letter to Ray and Gill Lycette, 15 August 1980
79 Atkin M, Letter to Ray and Gill Lycette, 24 October 1980
80 Atkin M, Letter to Ray and Gill Lycette, 12 April 1981

Chapter 5
81 Atkin M, Letter to Ray and Gill Lycette, 25 April 1981
82 Atkin M, Letter to Ray and Gill Lycette, 4 May 1981
83 Atkin M, Letter to Ray and Gill Lycette, 19 May 1981
84 Atkin M, Letter to Ray and Gill Lycette, 10 June 1981
85 Atkin M, Letter to Ray and Gill Lycette 13 June 1981
86 Atkin M, Letter to Ray and Gill Lycette 21 June 1981
87 Atkin M, Letter to Ray and Gill Lycette 22 July 1981
88 Atkin M, Letter to Ray and Gill Lycette, 31 August 1981
89 Atkin M, Letter to Ray and Gill Lycette, 6 September 1981

90 Atkin M, Letter to Ray and Gill Lycette, 4 October 1981
91 Atkin M, Letter to Ray and Gill Lycette, 26 October 1981
92 Atkin M, Letter to Ray and Gill Lycette, 1 November 1981
93 Atkin M, Letter to Ray and Gill Lycette, 12 November 1981
94 Atkin M, Letter to Ray and Gill Lycette, 23 November 1981
95 Atkin M, Letter to Ray and Gill Lycette, 12 December 1981
96 Atkin M, Letter to Ray and Gill Lycette, 7 January 1982
97 Atkin M. Letter to Ray and Gill Lycette, 10 January 1982
98 Atkin M. Letter to Ray and Gill Lycette 14 February 1982
99 Atkin M. Letter to Ray and Gill Lycette 20 March 1982
100 Atkin M. Letter to Ray and Gill Lycette 29 March 1982
101 Atkin M. Letter to Ray and Gill Lycette 2 April 1982
102 Atkin M. Letter to Ray and Gill Lycette 16 April 1982

Chapter 6

103 Atkin G. Letter to Ray Lycette 6 May 1982
104 Atkin M, Letter to Gill and Ray Lycette, 15 May 1982.
105 Atkin M, The *Sun*, January 1983
106 Moore C. 2013 see Bibliography
107 Ta'aimaesiburu A. 5 January 1983. Sahu. Recorded by Atkin M
108 Moore C. 2013 see bibliography Solomon Islands Encyclopaedia
109 Atkin M, Letter to Gill and Ray Lycette, 16 May 1982
110 Atkin M, Letter to Gill and Ray Lycette, 21 May 1982
111 Atkin M, Letter to Gill and Ray Lycette, 4 June 1982
112 Atkin M, Letter to Gill and Ray Lycette, 19 June 1982
113 Atkin M, Letter to Gill and Ray Lycette 12 July 1982
114 Atkin G, Toktok Praised at last, *Solomons Toktok*, p 2, 21 July 1982
115 Atkin M, Letter to Gill and Ray Lycette, 23 July 1982
116 Atkin M, General Nurse Training suspended, *Solomons Toktok*, p 2, 21 July 1982
117 Atkin M, Letter to Ray Lycette, Hong Kong, 27 July 1982
118 Atkin M, Letter to Gill Lycette, NZ, 27 July 1982
119 Atkin M, Honiara Primary Schools may turn away pupils in 1983, *Solomons Toktok*, Front page, 4 August 1982
120 Atkin M, Parents come and visit us pleads handicapped Centre, *Solomons Toktok*, p 11, 11 August 1982
121 Atkin M, Letter to Gill and Ray Lycette, 14 August 1982
122 Atkin M, Letter to Gill and Ray Lycette, 2 September 1982
123 Atkin G, Editorial Star congratulated, *Solomons Toktok*, 9 September 1982
124 Atkin M, Letter to Gill and Ray Lycette 11 October 1982
125 Atkin M, Letter to Gill and Ray Lycette 20 October 1982

126 Atkin M, Overpopulation worries Sir Peter, *Solomon Toktok*, p 3, 20 January 1983
127 Atkin M, Depo-Provera safe to use, Solomons Toktok, p 1, 17 February 1983
128 Atkin M, Women support family planning, Solomons Toktok, p 3-4, 26 May 1983
129 UNDP, Solomon Islands Youth Status Report, 2018 See Bibliography
130 Solomon Islands Central Bank, Annual Report 1982 as reported in the Sun, April 1983 p 8
131 UNDP, Solomon Islands Youth Status Report, 2018, see Bibliography
132 Solomon Islands Central Bank, Annual Report 1982 as reported in the Sun, April 1983 p 8
133 WHO, 2017 Solomon Islands Country Profile Malaria, see Bibliography
134 Atkin M, Fire in Chinatown, *The Sun*, Front page, February 1983
135 Atkin G, Editorial, The Sun, page five, February 1983
136 Atkin M, Police detain youth without a warrant, p 1, *Solomons Toktok*, 17 February 1983
137 Atkin M, Letter to Gill and Ray Lycette, 15 March 1983
138 Frazer 1997 in Kabutaulaka T T. Chapter 12, Solomon Islands Forestry and local ownership in Chapter 12, of Australian National University Conference, see Bibliography
139 Atkin M, Interview Prime Minister, p 8, April 1983
140 Atkin M, Solomons will face timber export shortage, p 1, 11 August 1983
141 Atkin M, Central Bank records low level investment, p 8, April 1983
142 Atkin M, Solomons Toktok, p 12, 19 May 1983
143 Westoby J. et.al 1976, see Bibliography
144 Atkin M, Study recommends forestry commission, *Solomons Toktok*, p 12, 14 May, 1983
145 Fiji Pine Commission, see Bibliography
146 Atkin M, Central Bank records record low investment, The Sun, p 8, April 1983
147 Atkin M, Government spends excessive money on Provincial Secondary Schools, p 6-7, Solomons Toktok, p6-7, 17 February 1983
148 Atkin M, Price Control chips off profits, *Solomons Toktok*, p 1-2, 26 May 1983
149 Lycette G, Letter to Diana Adams Smith May 1983

Chapter 7
150 Atkin M, Letter to Ray Lycette 16 August 1983
151 Atkin M, Hospital staff oppose Minister's intervention, p 1, *Solomons*

Toktok, 3 November 1983
152 Atkin M. Letter to Gill and Ray Lycette, 6 November 1983
153 Atkin M. Guadalcanal Province almost broke, p2, *Solomons Toktok*, 17 November 1983
154 Atkin M. Damaged trucks affect agricultural extension, p 2,4. *Solomons Toktok*, 17 Nov 1983
155 Atkin M. Editorial p 3, 17 November 1983
156 Atkin M. Mi Mere, p 8, 17 November 1983
157 Atkin M, Letter to Gill and Ray Lycette, 22 November 1983
158 Atkin M, Letter to Gill and Ray Lycette, 27 November 1983
159 Atkin M, Hasty marriage saves woman from deportation, p 1, *Solomons Toktok*, 24 November 1983
160 Atkin M, Editorial p 3, *Solomons Toktok*, 24 November 1983
161 Atkin M, Editorial p 3, *Solomons Toktok*, 24 November 1983
162 Atkin M, Anuha Resort opens, p 6,7,8, 24 November 1983
163 Atkin M, Drug case awaits High Court, p 11 *Solomons Toktok* 1 December 1983
164 Maukera R and Muga F, Tobacco, alcohol and marijuana use in Honiara students, 2018 see bibliography
165 Atkin M, Honiara Councillors request terminal grants. P 1, *Solomons Toktok*, 8 December 1983
166 Atkin M. Overseas trips overspent. P 1, *Solomons Toktok*, 8 December 1983
167 Atkin M, Letter to Gill and Ray Lycette, 13 December 1983
168 Atkin M, Chief Justice will be missed, p 3, *Solomons Toktok* 12 Jan 1984
169 Atkin G, Griffith Asia Institute, 27 April 2020. See Bibliography
170 Atkin M, Reflection, Unpublished, March 1984

Chapter 8
171 Atkin M, diary 16 March 1984
172 Atkin M, diary 21 March 1984
173 Atkin M, letter to Gill and Ray Lycette, 25 March 1984
174 Atkin M, diary 21st December 1992
175 Roughan J, Comment, p 3 *Solomon Voice*, 13 January 1992
176 Atkin M, diary 22 December 1992
177 Angiki D. letter Solomons Times, 26 June 2009 see Bibliography
178 Atkin J. diary 23 December 1992
179 Atkin M, diary 23 December 1992
180 Atkin B, Diary 24 December 1992
181 Atkin M, Diary 25 December 1992
182 Atkin J, Diary 25 December 1992
183 Atkin B, Diary 27 December 1992

184 Atkin J, Diary 27 December 1992
185 Atkin B, Diary 28 December 1992
186 Atkin M, Diary 29 December 1992
187 Atkin J, Diary 30 December 1992
188 Atkin M, Diary 30 December 1992
189 Atkin B, Diary 30 December 1992
190 Atkin B, Diary 1 January 1993
191 Atkin M, Diary 1 January 1993
192 Atkin M, Diary 2 January 1993
193 Atkin B, Diary 3 January 1993
194 Atkin M, Diary 3 January 1993
195 Atkin B, Diary 4 January 1993
196 Atkin M, Diary 8 January 1993
197 Atkin M, Diary 9 January 1993
198 Atkin M, Diary 10 January 1993
199 Atkin M, Diary 12 January 1993
200 Atkin J. Diary 12 January 1993
201 Atkin M, Diary 13 January 1993
202 Atkin M, Diary 13 January 1993
203 Atkin M, Diary 14 January 1993
204 Atkin M, Diary 14 January 1993
205 Atkin B, Diary 14 January 1993
206 Atkin M, Diary 16 January 1993
207 Atkin B, Diary 16 January 1993
208 Atkin B, Diary 17 January 1993

Chapter 9
209 Poten J. 9 October 1995, see Bibliography
210 Atkin M, Cervical cancer in the Solomon Islands, 1999, see Bibliography
211 Ministry of Health and Medical Services, *Solomon Islands Review* 1996, see Bibliography
212 Australian Institute of Health and Welfare 1996, see Bibliography
213 Family Planning NSW, Undated, see bibliography
214 Family Planning NSW, 2020, see bibliography

Chapter 10
215 Fraenkel J, 2005, *The Manipulation of Custom*.
216 Brown T, 2018 see bibliography
217 Roughan J (1993) Comment John Roughan, *Solomons Voice*
218 Brown T 2018, see Bibliography
219 Change to Fraenkel J, 2005, *The Manipulation of Custom*
220 Fraenkel J. 2005, The Manipulation of Custom, Pandanus Books, New

Ed
221 Dan G, 23 May 2014, Lowy Institute, see Bibliography
222 O'Callaghan M-L. 21 March 2001, 'The Stolen Nation,' *The Australian*
223 Atkin G. Letter to Margaret Atkin 7 May 2001
224 Fraenkel, J, 2005
225 Ibid
226 Ibid
227 ibid
228 Atkin M, Diary Solomons Visit, 16 December 2003 to 7 January 2004

Chapter 11
229 WHO 2006, see Bibliography
230 Kalinga Seneviratne, 22 April 2006 InterPress News, see Bibliography
231 Spiller Penny, 21 April 2006, BBC news, see Bibliography
232 Fraenkel J. 29 April, 2019, see Bibliography
233 Atkin M, Diary Solomon Islands May 2006
234 *Masalai tokout*, No 45, 27 April 2006, The Solomons, Logging corruption ruins a nation, see Bibliography.
235 Canfell K, 9 January 2017, Cancer Council see Bibliography
236 Atkin M, Diary November 2014
237 Atkin M, Diary 30 December 2014

Chapter 14
238 WHO Western Pacific 2018, see Bibliography
239 World Obesity Organisation 2021, taken from the International Diabetes Fed 2021, see Bibliography
240 ACCF 2021 see Bibliography
241 ACCF 2020, see Bibliography
242 FPNSW 2021, see Bibliography
243 WHO 2019, see Bibliography
244 RACP 2018, see Bibliography

Chapter 15
245 Atkin B. October 2021, Makira Gold website see Bibliography.
246 Byrne A. 8 June 2016, Australian High Commissioner, see Australian High Commission Bibliography
247 Australian High Commission Press Release 8 June 2016, see Bibliography
248 Strong Island Foundation 2021, see Bibliography
249 Lam L.T. 9 Jan 2020. Chocolate changes lives in Solomons SBS, see Bibliography

www.ingramcontent.com/pod-product-compliance
Lightning Source LLC
Chambersburg PA
CBHW051534010526
44107CB00064B/2724